Worshiping Well

A Mass Guide for Planners and Participants

Lawrence E. Mick

A Liturgical Press Book

 THE LITURGICAL PRESS
Collegeville, Minnesota

Cover design by Greg Becker

1	2	3	4	5	6	7	8

Library of Congress Cataloging-in-Publication Data

Mick, Lawrence E., 1946–
    Worshiping well : a mass guide for planners and participants / Lawrence E. Mick.
        p.   cm.
    ISBN 0-8146-2423-5
    1. Mass—Celebration.   2. Catholic Church—Liturgy.   I. Title.
BX2230.2.M45   1997
264'.0203—dc21
                                        96-29593
                                           CIP

Contents

Preface

It has been more than twenty-five years since we began using the current Order of Mass, yet the challenge of implementing it fully and celebrating it well continues. It seems opportune to review periodically the different parts and various options contained in the rite. In this book, we will look at the Mass in some detail, seeking a deeper understanding of this central worship experience and looking at ways to improve the experience in parish communities.

The bulk of the material in this book first saw the light of day as a series of articles in *Today's Parish* magazine during 1993, 1994, and 1995. Daniel Connors, the magazine's editor, recognizes the value of returning regularly to the foundational rites that shape parish worship and life in order to understand them more fully and implement them more effectively. The articles provided readers of the magazine an opportunity to review, step by step, their own parish's worship.

Such a review invariably raises questions: How well have we understood the changes that we've experienced? How well have we implemented those changes? What mistakes have we made in using the new ritual order? What is the history and background of each part of the Mass? Have we made full use of the options allowed in the current liturgical books? Should we have other options? Do we need a whole new Order of Mass? How could we improve the experience of Sunday worship for the majority of parishioners? What steps might a parish take to begin a revival of liturgical renewal on the local level? Addressing such questions is the focus of this book.

Much effort has been expended over the past quarter-century in most parishes to make Sunday worship a better and more powerful experience. While undoubtedly there have been missteps and excesses, the vast majority of these efforts have borne fruit and fostered the spiritual growth of many. Some of these efforts have pushed beyond the official rites, using local creativity to find new ways to express the praises of God. But much of what has been done or remains to be done involves the careful and thoughtful implementation of the official rites as they have been set forth in the Sacramentary and the Lectionary and in other liturgical books and documents. Returning to the basics is always essential to renewal, and a review of those basics can help us to evaluate what has been done or might be done to foster continued growth in the liturgical renewal on the parish level.

In this book, I will stay very close to the official rites and guidelines that we have received. My bias is that we would be much farther along the path of genuine liturgical renewal if every parish made the effort simply to implement the official rites fully. At the same time, it is important to have a balanced view of liturgical rules and rubrics. Such a balance is possible only when it is recognized that while some rules are central to the ritual, others are more peripheral. Good pastoral sensitivity not only allows for, but sometimes demands, adaptations of the liturgical rites. But such adaptations must flow from solid liturgical principles that are based upon an understanding of the history and purpose of the ritual element being considered and the theological issues involved. Good liturgical practice is neither the result of slavish adherence to every detail of the rubrics nor a matter of free creativity without regard to history, theology, or the practice of the wider church. As usual in such matters, virtue stands in the middle. This volume will attempt to provide at least the basic understanding needed for proper implementation of the current Order of Mass, as well as a basis for understanding future changes that will no doubt occur as liturgical renewal unfolds. As this volume goes to press, some revisions of the Order of Mass in the new Sacramentary are making their way through the long approval process. Such proposed changes will be noted as we go along.

CHAPTER 1

The Church: People Who Worship

Beyond the Liturgy

When the Second Vatican Council began its work of renewing the Church, it began with the Constitution on the Sacred Liturgy. This reflected an expectation that the renewal of the liturgy would lead to the broader renewal of all of church life. This was in accord with the hopes of the promoters of liturgical renewal in the decades before the council, both in this country and around the world. Those pioneers of liturgical formation and renewal had a broad vision that linked renewed worship experiences with a renewed spirituality leading to a renewal of church life and ultimately of society as a whole. Issues of church renewal and social justice were clearly linked in the writings of these men and women, who believed that the renewal of society could only be achieved through a renewal of the Church, which in turn required a renewed worship.

But something strange happened when the mandate for reform came from the bishops of the Second Vatican Council. Perhaps because we were so unaware of the efforts of reformers both in Europe and in the United States, most parishes in this country began to work on liturgical renewal without a strong sense of the necessary links with the renewal of church structures and efforts for social justice. A variety of authors and speakers in recent years have called us back to that integrated vision, but we have a long way to go before such a vision is shared by the majority of those who gather each Sunday for worship in our parishes.

One of the results of the rapid increase in available knowledge that is called the "information explosion" is that we are forced to specialize. So in this book we will focus on our ritual life and only on the most central of our sacraments at that. But liturgy does not exist in a vacuum, and true liturgical renewal cannot occur without significant attention to the broader issues of church life and the social/cultural context which influences our worship. The linkage goes in both directions: the liturgy should lead us to a spiritual renewal that impels us to evangelize the world and make Christ's love evident to all, but the renewal of the liturgy itself requires a renewed spirit that can confront those influences of our culture and our history that impede the full celebration of our rituals.

So as we look at the various parts of the Mass, we will also attempt to suggest some implications of those rites for the rest of our living and to uncover some of the deeper questions that we must confront if a true renewal of our worship is ever to occur. Whenever we probe our life of worship, we are sure to discover broader issues about the way we live our life as Church and how we adopt or challenge the ways of the world. Liturgy and life are not two separate realms. Our worship is shaped by and also shapes the rest of our life.

A Symphony in Four Movements

Before we begin to look at the individual rituals and prayers that make up the liturgy of the Eucharist, it may be helpful to step back and get an overall view of the celebration. Any human celebration generally involves four elements:

1. A gathering of those who will celebrate together
2. Communication between those assembled, taking a variety of forms
3. Shared ritual, commonly involving food and drink
4. Some kind of leave taking or dismissal

These four elements occur in an infinite variety of forms, ranging from a child's imaginary tea party to a formal banquet, from a teen party to a presidential inauguration. Whenever humans celebrate, we gather, we speak, we share, and we disperse.

In the Eucharist these four elements define the four sections of the ritual. We begin with gathering rites, formally called the Introductory or Entrance Rites. We speak the meaning of our gathering and of our lives in the Liturgy of the Word. Then we share a ritual meal in the Liturgy of the Eucharist. When the celebration ends, we take leave of one another in the Concluding or Dismissal Rite. The Entrance and Concluding Rites are subordinate to the Liturgy of the Word and Eucharist, but each section has its purpose and importance. The liturgy as a whole is somewhat like a symphony, with moments of high concentration interwoven with times of lesser intensity. Recognition of the purpose of each section of the Mass and attention to the structure and rhythm of the ritual itself is required for proper preparation and full participation. We cannot randomly change and radically restructure our rituals of worship without doing violence to their meaning, any more than we can change the shape and rhythm of a symphony without destroying the integrity of the piece.

An Assembly, Not an Audience

At the same time, it must also be noted that our worship differs from a symphony in that the particular assembly gathered for worship does and should influence the particular shape and tone of the ritual experience. A symphony orchestra in Germany might be expected to play a Mozart symphony in much the same way as an orchestra in Chicago, with only minor variations in interpretation of the music. But the Roman Mass celebrated in Germany would be quite different in many respects from the same ritual celebrated in Chicago. Not only the language and the choice of hymns would be expected to differ, but the tone of the celebration might be different in a variety of ways because of differences in the culture and make-up of the respective assemblies of worshippers.

This point reminds us of the centrality of the assembly in the liturgy of the Mass. The role of the assembly in our renewed worship is perhaps the main factor that we need to examine if we are to breathe new life into the liturgical renewal in our own time. In the recent past, the role of the assembly was defined primarily in terms of being physically present. As long as people attended Mass, they fulfilled their obligation. The responsibility for the celebration of the ritual was placed entirely on the priest presider. The Mass was seen as his act of worship which the congregation shared only minimally and from a distance.

The renewal of the liturgy has as its stated goal the full, conscious, active participation of all the faithful in liturgical celebrations (cf. Constitution on the Sacred Liturgy [CSL], #14). The Second Vatican Council insists that pastors have a "duty to ensure that the faithful take part fully aware of what they are doing, actively engaged in the rite, and enriched by its effects" (CSL, #11). There is no question that in the past two decades the level of participation has increased significantly for most of those who gather for Sunday Eucharist. Yet old attitudes and understandings die hard, and it must also be admitted that changes in external behavior do not always result in interior renewal. Many people seem to be following the new guidelines for the celebration of the Eucharist and the other sacraments without having caught the new vision that underlies those guidelines. Most worshippers on Sunday morning seem largely unaware of their own responsibility for the quality of the community's worship. They assume that good worship is someone else's responsibility, primarily the presider and perhaps the musicians or the worship committee. But liturgy is the work of all the members of the assembly. It is not a spectator sport, but a corporate act of prayer and praise that requires the active engagement of every member of the assembly. So long as worship is seen as the responsibility of a few, our liturgy will limp. Only when every member of the assembly understands his or her importance and accepts the responsibility for creating good worship will the vision of Vatican II come to fruition.

Those Who Gather

The first concern, therefore, of those who prepare parish liturgies must be the people who form the assembly. All those who gather for a given celebration of the Eucharist are the ministers of the Eucharist. They make a life-giving celebration happen or they impede it. Some members of the assembly take special roles of service within the celebration: lectors, ushers, Eucharistic ministers, musicians, acolytes, choir, presider, etc. But every member of the assembly shares the ministry of the Eucharist. They are the primary means of the presence of Christ during the celebration. They form the Body of Christ, and it is Christ himself who ultimately offers worship to the Father, Christ himself who offers the sacrifice.

The Second Vatican Council reminded us that Christ is present in the Eucharist in at least four different ways: Christ is present in the assembly—"For where two or three are gathered in my name, there am I in their midst" (Matt 18:20). Christ is present in the priest who leads the assembly in worship. When the word of God is proclaimed in Scripture and preaching within the assembly, Christ speaks today. And Christ is present in the bread and wine shared in the Eucharistic meal.

We Catholics have been very aware of Christ's presence under the form of bread and wine. The presence of Christ through the presider has long been recognized by the faithful. And we are learning to respect the word proclaimed as Christ speaking to us in our own time. But the first and most fundamental presence, the presence of Christ in the assembly itself, is all too often overlooked. We do not seem to be very good at recognizing Christ in one another.

Part of this is simply the result of past training which focused almost exclusively on the presence of Christ in the form of bread and wine, often even concentrating more on the presence of Christ in the tabernacle than on his presence during the Mass itself. But part of the problem also seems to be a lack of awareness among many of the faithful of the dignity of their own status as baptized members of the Body of Christ. Most Catholics expect the priest to be a minister of Christ, a channel for Christ's presence and grace. They are not as quick to expect Christ to be present through themselves or their fellow parishioners. We need to help all members of our assemblies to claim their rightful dignity. They form the Body of Christ. Christ has chosen to be present in the world through them. They are called to be channels of grace and a means of Christ's presence both in worship and in daily life. Helping our brothers and sisters to reclaim their status in the Church may be the most important step we can take in renewing our liturgical life. While we take our tour through the various rituals and prayers that make up our celebration of the Eucharist, it is important to remember these words from the U.S. bishop's document *Environment and Art in Catholic Worship:* "Among the symbols with which liturgy deals, none is more important than this assembly of believers" (#28).

Questions for Reflection and Discussion

1. What memories do you have of the liturgy before the Second Vatican Council? What was your initial reaction to the changes in the liturgy after the council?

2. What were the most significant of the liturgical changes for you? In what way did they affect your spiritual life?

3. How well does your community celebrate the liturgy? What do you think are your strong points? What needs the most improvement?

4. What connections do you recognize between the liturgy and the mission of the Church in the world? What helps you to link your daily life with your worship?

5. How clear do you think the four parts of the Mass are to the people of your community? What might help them to recognize these different movements?

6. How aware is your average Sunday assembly of the importance of their role in the liturgy? What percentage do you think just attend? What percentage take responsibility for

creating good worship? How can the assembly's self-awareness be heightened?

7. How well is the parish forming the next generation—in school, in religious education programs, in family activities—to be active participants in worship? What steps could be taken to lead them more fully into the spirit of the liturgy?

8. Do you find it easy or difficult to recognize the presence of Christ in other people? What helps or hinders that recognition? Is it easier or harder to recognize his presence in the presider at worship? How do you think the community as a whole responds to Christ's presence in these modes?

9. Does your community respond to the Liturgy of the Word as an experience of Christ speaking to us today? Why or why not?

10. Do you think most people in your community recognize Christ in the bread and wine shared? Do they believe the bread and wine are truly his body and blood? Do they recognize that communion in Christ involves communion with all the members of his body?

CHAPTER 2

Becoming an Assembly for Worship

According to the *General Instruction of the Roman Missal*, which is printed in the front of the Sacramentary, the purpose of the Entrance Rites of the Mass is "that the faithful coming together take on the form of a community and prepare themselves to listen to God's word and celebrate the Eucharist properly (#24). The second goal, that of preparing to listen and celebrate properly, is dependent on the first, taking on the form of a community. The Eucharist is a communal act of worship, not a private or individual act, and to celebrate it properly, those who gather must enter into an organic unity that enables them to function as the one Body of Christ, united with Christ their head in offering the sacrifice of praise to the Father.

This fact, which is so fundamental to proper celebration of the Eucharist, is unfortunately largely unrecognized by many, if not most, of those who assemble each Sunday for worship. This is not surprising when we consider our recent worship experience. The celebration of the Mass for centuries prior to the Second Vatican Council was a "spectator sport" at best. All that was really expected of the assembly is that they be physically present. Once in attendance, one could follow the priest's Latin prayers with a personal missal, say the Rosary, read other books or say other prayers. It was a very individualistic experience, at least as far as external participation is concerned. A thousand people could be gathered in the same church building for Mass, with each of them "doing their own thing" spiritually and with minimal interaction with those around them. Such interaction, in fact, was positively discouraged by strictures against talking in church or even looking around to see who was sitting or kneeling behind you. All attention was to be focused on God, visualized as being in heaven, or on Christ in the tabernacle. The spiritual mode was one-to-one relationship between Jesus and the individual.

At the same time, it should be noted that there was often an unspoken sense of community identity, even though it was not expressed ritually during worship. Many parishes were the center of life for their congregations; in this country, many parishes were the focal points of ethnic communities who shared both their Catholic faith and their immigrant identity. This religious communal identity, born of an integration between faith and daily life, no doubt provided an underlying sense of unity with all those who gathered on Sunday. They were the same people with whom one gathered for education, for socializing, for community action, and for celebrating births, marriages, and deaths.

Obstacles to Communal Identity

That sense of communal identity began to dissipate with the development of suburbia and the increasing economic success of Catholic families. In most cases, the Church ceased to be the focal point for people's daily lives, becoming primarily a place for Sunday worship and perhaps for parochial education. The old close-knit ethnic Catholic communities have largely disappeared, and church membership now often links one with thousands of relative strangers.

The reform of the liturgy following the Second Vatican Council presumes a strong community identity and a communal engagement in worship. Several things have conspired to prevent the development of such community, however. There was not adequate recognition at the beginning that the new liturgy required some radically new attitudes and approaches to worship. Most church leaders knew that we were shifting from an individual to a communal form of worship, and there was much talk about "community." But there was a lot of naïveté, about how such community could be fostered. Some wanted to simply assume the existence of a community ready for worship, sometimes counting on the past ethnic parish identity to provide what was needed. Others assumed that the liturgy itself would produce such a community, a hope that has disappointed many.

At the same time, in our American cultural situation, strong currents of hyper-individualism were changing our social and personal perspectives. The council and its reforms coincided with the upheaval of the sixties and seventies and the subsequent reaction of the "me-generation" in the eighties. The American political and social experiment has always stressed individual rights and freedoms. No other civilization in history has so exalted the individual, and this is probably our greatest gift to the world as a society. But any good thing can be overdone, and recent years have seen such an emphasis on the individual that our society has lost any viable sense of community and the common good. Advertising, the entertainment media, pop psychology, music, and the political process have all reflected an intense individualism that leaves little room for corporate identity or activity for the common good. There are a few hints that things may be starting to change, but for years we have been fed a steady diet of self-centeredness and selfishness. I have asked numerous groups how long it has been since they heard a politician, national or local, ask them to sacrifice personal desires for the common good, and the consistent answer is the early sixties when President Kennedy said, "Ask not what your country can do for you, but what you can do for your country." There was some hint of this kind of challenge after the 1992 presidential election, but negative public reaction led President Clinton to give up using the word "sacrifice" soon after his inauguration.

There are multiple implications of this overdeveloped stress on the individual, but our concern here is with worship. The cultural lack of awareness of the common good and of our essential links to one another is devastating to Christian worship. To enter into one corporate act of sacrifice and praise requires a willingness to surrender some of our independence. We have to be willing to become part of something larger than ourselves, and that means we must be willing to give up many of our personal preferences. The Eucharist is not Burger King, and we can't always have it our way. Christian worship, like all of Christian life, calls us to give of ourselves to others. It requires putting the needs of others first and asking what we can give more than what we can receive from worship: Ask not what the Mass can do for you, but what you can do for the Mass!

The Ministry of Hospitality

The fundamental issue here is one of hospitality. Fr. Eugene Walsh used to insist that hospitality means saying that for the time we are together, "there is room for you in my life." He said that we aren't really a family at worship; we are much too large a group for that. And the demands of life being what they are, we may not be able to devote ourselves all week long to those who gather with us at worship on Sunday. But hospitality is essential to good worship, and it means making room in our lives and our hearts for our fellow worshippers while we are together.

Hospitality is the basic ministry needed in order for the Entrance Rites to have any chance of achieving their goal. We spend most of our lives apart from those with whom we worship. To enter into a communal act at Eucharist, we have to find ways to reconnect when we gather. We need an attitude of openness to others and willingness to join together in Christ to offer prayer and praise to the Father.

The issue of hospitality, however, can easily be misunderstood. It is much more than a matter of good manners or an attempt to produce a folksy informality at church. Ultimately it is a matter of recognizing and responding to the presence of Christ in our midst. As the council reminded us, Christ is truly present whenever we gather in his name. Responding to that presence is a basic matter of reverence.

A Question of Reverence

There have been numerous complaints voiced since the council that we have lost a sense of reverence at Mass. There may be some truth to the charge, and it is no doubt linked to the general decline in reverence and respect for all institutions and individuals in our culture. But part of the problem is that we do not recognize that reverence can be manifested in various ways. In the recent past, reverence was primarily signaled in negative ways: by not talking in church, not entering the sanctuary, not touching the chalice, etc. Today we are called to find new ways to express reverence, ways that perhaps are better attuned to an incarnational theology which recognizes that God can be found in the most humble and ordinary things and people, not just within majestic spaces and high rituals.

But the first step of reverence is recognition of the presence of God. If Christ is present in our very gathering, if Christ truly dwells in each of us, then reverence demands that we recognize and respond to that presence. Thus, hospitality in Christian worship, like most human realities in worship, has a far deeper significance than simple good manners or friendliness. It is a matter of responding to the very presence of the divine in our midst. We have been very good about recognizing the divine presence in the reserved sacrament in the tabernacle; we have not been so good at recognizing the presence of Christ in one another. Many people of all religions have been edified by the ministry of Mother Teresa of Calcutta. What we also need is the faith that leads her to such ministry; she says she is able to minister to dying beggars from the streets of Calcutta because when she looks at each of them she sees the face of Christ. This should be even more true when we look upon our brothers and sisters in the faith, for Christ dwells in us through the grace of baptism, and together we form his very Body.

Many parishes have attempted to improve the atmosphere of hospitality by getting ushers to greet all who come or by establishing greeters to perform that service. Other parishes have asked the presider to have everyone greet those around them before Mass begins; some parishes have even moved the sign of peace to the beginning of Mass, an unfortunate but understandable decision. All of these efforts may be helpful beginnings, but the goal must be for all members of the assembly to learn to be hospitable to one another. It should not depend on the presider or a small group of designated greeters; every member of the assembly has the responsibility to help create a welcoming community, to recognize the presence of Christ in all who gather, and to respond to that presence with genuine care and concern.

The danger, of course, is that attempts to foster hospitality at worship will degenerate into shallow congeniality with conversations about the latest sports game, the weather, and other similar cocktail party topics. What is called for is a reverent concern for one another, inquiring after sick family members, offering support for one seeking employment, sharing how the Lord has touched our lives this week, offering sympathy to the grieving, welcoming visitors to the parish, etc. True hospitality presumes a true love of neighbor that results in a true concern and care; such is the conversation that is appropriate before the Eucharist begins, not mere talk to pass the time.

Learning to talk in church will be difficult for those well-trained in their youth to keep silence. Since this is seen as an issue of reverence, what is needed is education about the various ways that Christ is present and the ways we can show reverence for each. The process is helped by having the tabernacle in a separate chapel of reservation, as the liturgical documents have recommended for some years now. Parishes fortunate enough to have a large gathering space outside the main worship space might foster hospitality there, but most parishes will need to learn that recognizing the presence of Christ in one another is precisely the reverence required of us as we gather in the worship space and seek to become an assembly prepared for worship.

Beginning in the Parking Lot

Before the Entrance Rites formally begin, there is much that must happen if those gathering are to become a true assembly of God, one people united as the Body of Christ, prepared to listen to the word of God as it is proclaimed in the community and to celebrate the Eucharistic meal that both expresses and strengthens their unity. Parish planners need to pay attention to what happens in the parking lot, on the sidewalks, at the doors, in the vestibule, and in the worship space before the Mass begins. Efforts aimed at helping people to learn to recognize the presence of the Lord wherever two or three are gathered in his name will bear good fruit for worship.

For example, worship committee members or greeters might station themselves in the parking lot in good weather to greet people even before they reach the doors of the church. One parish even had greeters dressed as clowns in the parking lot on a special occasion; it brought a lot of smiles and good conversation and thus helped form the community. Parishes might evaluate the outdoor area of the church property to see if it is hospitable and fosters a sense of peace and beauty. Some parishes have created small but attractive gardens through which parishioners pass as they enter church. Others have found ways to decorate with banners, streamers, wreaths, etc. on the outside of the church and/or in the vestibule so that the spirit of the feast or season is evident even before people enter the worship space.

Once people enter, of course, they should be encouraged to express the Christian love that binds them to one another. The best encouragement is the example of the presider, ushers, planners, and other parishioners who simply but sincerely welcome them warmly, ask after their health, greet the children, and express their joy at being together again. A few people doing this quietly in the worship space itself will, over a period of time, lead others to do the same. A reverent and genuine caring is contagious, and the example of parish leaders doing this will give others the permission they need to break the absolute silence in church.

The goals of the Entrance Rites are important, but they cannot be achieved by the ritual words and actions in isolation. Their fulfillment depends on people who know what their role in worship requires and who are willing to give of themselves to create a life-giving Eucharist that offers fitting praise to God.

When we were children, we learned that when buttoning a shirt or blouse, it is important to begin with the right button at the bottom or else it will not come out right at the top. So, too, with worship: if we want it to come out right, we have to begin correctly. What happens as we gather can significantly foster or impede the spiritual power and beauty of the rest of the Mass.

Questions for Reflection and Discussion

1. What is the difference between people gathered in the same place to do their own praying and people engaged in one communal act of prayer? Do you find it easy or difficult to enter into a communal act of worship?

2. How would you evaluate your community's ability to enter into communal liturgy? Are they eager to praise God together or are they more interested in private prayer at church? How can people be led to enter more fully into the communal action?

3. What do you think is the biggest obstacle to developing a deeper communal identity at worship? How can this obstacle be confronted?

4. How much do you think American politics and popular culture have affected our attitudes toward church and worship? Can you see positive effects as well as negative ones?

5. How hospitable is your worshiping community—toward one another, toward strangers?

6. What kind of conversations occur in your community as people gather for worship? Do they help people sense the presence of Christ in others, or are they just a distraction? How could healthy sharing be encouraged?

7. What greets you when you arrive at church? Is there hospitality in the parking lot? Are the entrances of the building pleasant and peaceful?

8. How could your community extend decoration and symbols of the feasts and seasons beyond the sanctuary to help shape the assembly's gathering?

9. Do people greet one another at church? Is this left only to the ushers or a corps of greeters, or is it truly a welcoming community?

10. What is the first step your community might take at this point to encourage more hospitality as people gather for worship?

CHAPTER 3

Entrance Rites:
Our Complicated Beginning

One of the most important things to remember about liturgical renewal is that it is a work in progress. This is true in two senses: first, the renewal mandated by Vatican II is a long-term journey that we are far from completing; and second, our liturgy is a living thing that is always developing and changing as the world and the Church develop and change. One of the false expectations raised by years of what seemed to be unchanging liturgical rites is the belief that after the reform, things will settle down and the changes will be finished. That expectation is false because it rests on the assumption that our worship patterns are normally settled and unchanging. In fact, our liturgy has always been a living, and thus a changing, thing. The period between the Council of Trent and the Second Vatican Council was really an abnormal period, with less than the normal rate of change, though some changes occurred even during those centuries.

A good example of the degree of change in worship patterns that takes place over time can be found in the Entrance Rites of the Mass. The Introductory Rites, as we have them today, are the result of centuries of change and reform and compromise. Knowing something of the history of these rites can help us understand them today and perhaps make better use of them.

From Simplicity to Complexity

The German liturgist Anton Baumstark is noted for his principle of liturgical development: the more important the feast, the less it changes through the centuries. An example of this is our Good Friday service, which begins the way most liturgies began in the early centuries. After the people have gathered for worship, we pause (and prostrate) for silent prayer. Then a brief collect summarizes those prayers before the readings are proclaimed.

It is a long way from the simplicity of that beginning to the complexity of our current Entrance Rites. Remembering that liturgical developments occurred at different times and in different ways in various places, let us look at a simplified history of how our current rites developed. The early Church met in homes in small groups, so the need for formal entrance rites was minimal. After people gathered, when it was time to begin, the deacon or presider would call the assembly to order. All would spend a few moments in silent prayer and then begin the Liturgy of the Word. Early on, a brief spoken prayer was added to summarize the silent prayers of all; this opening prayer was called the collect, because it "collected" the quiet prayers of the assembly.

After Constantine legalized the Christian religion, he had basilicas built over the tomb of Peter and at other important Christian sites. These basilicas, like many European cathedrals today, had no pews and hence had no aisles. When it was time for the celebration to begin, the bishop needed to move from the back of the church, through the assembled throng, to the front. One good way to alert an assembly (or any crowd) that something is happening is through music, so an entrance song was introduced to accompany the procession from the back to the front. Perhaps the hymn also covered the commotion of the deacons as they went ahead of the procession to move people aside to create an aisle! One of the hymns commonly used for this entrance procession we now know as the Glory to God.

The next addition came some centuries later, at a time when the liturgy was becoming more clericalized and the assembly was seen as less and less important. The attitude developed that if the presider wasn't doing something, nothing of value was going on. So the presider was given prayers to say as he approached the altar. Those who are old enough to remember the pre-Vatican II Mass will remember the Prayers at the Foot of the Altar, which began with Psalm 42 and the refrain "I will go in to the altar of God." Originally, these were not prayers *at* the foot of the altar but prayers to *get* to the foot of the altar.

As the involvement of the assembly decreased, the opening song was taken over by a choir, and often one of the psalms was used as the entrance song. Over time, more elaborate music was developed for this choir piece, which was eventually shortened to a single verse, lest it go on too long. This is the origin of the *Introit* verse used in the pre-Vatican II Mass—still printed in the Sacramentary.

The decrease in the assembly's participation in the worship went hand-in-hand with an increasing sense of unworthiness before God. We see this reflected in a variety of manifestations, both ritually and artistically. For the Entrance Rite, it meant the addition of other prayers for the priest to say as he approached the altar, expressing his unworthiness to do so. These prayers included the *Confiteor* (I confess) and were said only by the priest, not by the assembly. This was the origin of what we now know as the penitential rite.

Recent Changes

In our own century, the developments continued. Before the Second Vatican Council, there were movements to increase congregational participation through Latin-English missals and through the *Missa Recitata,* in which the people recited the Latin responses. This was the first time the penitential prayers were said by the whole assembly. Also before the council there were some efforts at congregational singing of hymns during the Low Mass. Then after the council, as we began to celebrate the Mass in our own language, an opening hymn was added to an already complicated Entrance Rite. For a brief period, we really had three entrance songs: an entrance hymn, the old introit, and the Glory to God. Soon directives were issued that allowed the *Introit* to be omitted when an entrance song was sung.

This brief historical overview reminds us that our current Entrance Rites are a compilation of many centuries of developments. When the commission preparing the Order of Mass after Vatican II set to work, one of its primary principles was to remove some of the many layers of ritual and texts that had accumulated over the centuries, so that the basic structure and meaning of the rites would be more evident. The Entrance Rites which we have currently are a compromise between those who wanted a much simpler entrance, closer to our early church practice, and those who wanted to retain the various elements that had been added through history. Thus, for example, the penitential elements were shortened, but a penitential rite was retained.

Unfortunately, the practical result of these compromises is an Entrance Rite that Ralph Keifer has fittingly called our "cluttered vestibule." There are so many different elements to get through before we reach the Liturgy of the Word that the basic functions of these rites are hindered. Rather than preparing us to listen to the Word proclaimed, these complex rites may leave us ready for a break to take a breather!

A Challenge for Planners

One of the basic principles for liturgy planners, therefore, is to prepare the Entrance Rites in a way that minimizes the overload. If a parish were to employ all the elements possible in their fullest form, the order might look like this:

— a lengthy entrance song, with all verses sung
— the sign of the cross
— a greeting by the presider
— an invitation to repentance, followed by an extended silence
— the *Confiteor* (I confess)
— a sung *Kyrie* (Lord, have mercy)
— a lengthy sung *Gloria* (Glory to God)
— an invitation to prayer, followed by generous silence
— the opening prayer

That's a lot to do just to get started, and it's a very long way from the pattern we use on Good Friday! Rather than eagerness to hear the word, such an introductory rite might well produce a sense of exhaustion. Such a lengthy order is out of balance with the other parts of the Mass; the Entrance Rites are a minor section when compared to the Liturgy of the Word or the Liturgy of the Eucharist. Though it may be a bit more important and thus a bit longer than the Concluding Rite, it still should remain clearly introductory and not take on a life of its own.

The "Directory for Masses with Children," issued just a few years after the Order of Mass, recognized that the complexity of the Entrance Rites could be a problem for children. It notes that

> [t]he introductory rite of the Mass has as its purpose "that the faithful coming together take on the form of a community and prepare themselves to listen to God's word and celebrate the Eucharist properly." Therefore every effort should be made to create this disposition in the children and not to jeopardize it by an excess of rites in this part of the Mass.
>
> It is sometimes proper to omit one or other element of the introductory rite or perhaps to expand one of the elements. There should always be at least some introductory element, which is completed by the opening prayer. In choosing individual elements, care should be taken that each one be used from time to time and that none be entirely neglected. (#40)

For several years now, many experts and local planners have asked why this flexibility is allowed only in Masses with many children, since it seems that such adjustments would be very helpful to most Sunday assemblies of adults as well. In 1986, the International Commission on English in the Liturgy conducted a broad consultation on the Order of Mass. Of all the pastoral responses they received, the Introductory Rites drew the most comments. "Those who remarked on the introductory rites commented in general on their complexity, the confusion of purpose and moods of the various elements, the seeming predominance of the penitential aspect, and the historical novelty of the introductory rites as arranged at present" (*Second Progress Report on the Revision of the Roman Missal*, p. 93).

In response to these pastoral concerns, the International Commission on English in the Liturgy has proposed an approach to the Introductory Rites based on approved editions of other language groups, especially the German, French, and Italian missals. In this proposed approach, between the initial greeting and the opening prayer, a community would use one of six options on a given day. These six are: 1) blessing and sprinkling of water, 2) penitential rite, 3) litany of praise, which is what we know as Form C of the current penitential rite, 4) a sung *Kyrie,* 5) a sung Glory to God, or 6) other special rites for special occasions, such as a baptism, Passion Sunday procession, etc.

At this writing, this proposal has been approved by the U.S. bishops, with a minor change allowing the Glory to God to be used with one of the other opening rites if desired. This decision still must be approved by Rome. The process of approval is a lengthy one, and it remains to be seen when the new Sacramentary will be ready for parish use. So, the question is what to do while we wait for the new book.

Planners can take various steps to address the problem of our cluttered vestibule within the current guidelines. Choices need to be made about which elements to emphasize on a given Sunday. During Lent, for example, the penitential rite might be stressed, while the Glory to God is omitted. The U.S. bishops have approved an option in the new Sacramentary for the assembly to kneel for the penitential rite during Lent; many parishes have been doing this already to emphasize the rite. During Easter and on other great feasts, the Glory to God can be sung, while the shortest form of the penitential rite (Form B) is used. Or the penitential rite might be replaced by the blessing and sprinkling with water. Some parishes have tried singing the Glory to God during the sprinkling rather than beginning it after that rite is completed, though it might be best to use music that is linked to the sprinkling itself. Other parishes have chosen to use the Glory to God as the entrance song, either moving it forward or beginning with a silent procession, followed by the greeting and penitential rite and then singing the Glory to God. When there is a baptism at Mass, the introductory rites of the baptism, (asking the name, signing with the cross) replace the penitential rite. A similar decision is appropriate whenever there are special rites at the beginning of Mass.

A key issue in preparing the Entrance Rites is the use of music. There is no one ideal arrangement, but planners should be careful not to sing too many different parts of these introductory rites at any given Mass. Otherwise, this section will again be longer and more impressive than its relative importance in the Mass deserves. Music always emphasizes a text. A good entrance song should not extend too long, especially if the Glory to God is to be sung shortly thereafter. This does not mean singing only some verses of the entrance song, but choosing a song that is complete in a few verses. On a day when nothing else in the Entrance Rite is sung, a longer opening hymn may be appropriate. In Lent, an opening hymn might be omitted and the penitential rite might be sung. When the rite of sprinkling is planned, a song there might suggest beginning without an entrance song or using the Glory to God to accompany the sprinkling. Various combinations are possible; the goal is a balance that allows music to emphasize the particular part of the Introductory Rites that is being stressed that Sunday.

In the next chapter, we will revisit these rites in more detail, to see how best to make use of the various options within each section of these introductory rituals. Don't forget, however, that these rites can only do their job well if attention is being paid to the hospitality of the assembly as people gather, even before the first note of the entrance song is sounded!

Questions for Reflection and Discussion

1. What is your personal reaction to the idea that liturgy will continue to change and develop? Do you think most members of your community expect our worship to continue to change? Do they welcome such change or generally resist it?

2. What did you find most interesting about the historical development of the Entrance Rites? Is it helpful to know how they developed?

3. Do you find the Entrance Rites to be too long, too short, or about right? Do they fulfill their function of forming us into a community and preparing us to hear the word of God?

4. What is your reaction to the changes in the Entrance Rites approved by our bishops?

5. If you were invited to propose changes in the Entrance Rites, what would you recommend? Why?

6. Does your community vary the Introductory Rites for different occasions and seasons? Is varying emphasis put on different elements at different times?

7. How many parts of the Entrance Rites are normally sung in your community? Do you find it generally to be too much music, too little, or about right?

8. Is the Glory to God regularly sung in your community? Why or why not? Is reciting it effective or is it better omitted if it is not sung?

CHAPTER 4

A Walk Through the Vestibule

Now let's take a stroll slowly through the "cluttered vestibule" of the Entrance Rites to see how we might best make use of these various elements with which we begin our worship.

The Entrance Song

Ordinarily, we begin our worship with an opening song. This song is an important ritual action which has two main purposes. Singing together is itself a unifying act, and the entrance song calls the whole assembly to enter into our common act of worship. Since it is the first element of the celebration, the entrance song should also suggest the focus of the celebration. This is not to say that every Mass must have a narrow theme that should be clearly expressed in the opening song, but our limited human minds cannot celebrate the whole of the mystery of Christ at once. So each Mass does focus on one or several aspects of that mystery, and the opening song should give at least a hint of what is to come. So this song should be chosen according to the liturgical season, the feast, and/or the Scripture readings of the day. A Marian song to begin a Sunday Mass during Easter is not appropriate, even if it is during May. But a Marian song on a Marian feast may be just right.

If the entrance song is to serve its unifying function for the assembly, it needs to be a song that everyone can sing wholeheartedly. That means it generally should not be a new song that is unfamiliar to many in the assembly. If a new song suitable for entrance is to be introduced, it should be taught well over several weeks, and perhaps used during the Preparation of the Gifts once or twice until the assembly is comfortable with it. To use an opening song that people find difficult (and thus unpleasant) to sing is a sure way to discourage the enthusiasm that should mark the beginning of our common worship.

The length of the opening song is sometimes a matter of dispute. Many parishes never sing more than two verses of any song. Some writers insist that, since this song accompanies the entrance procession, it should stop as soon as the presider has reached the chair. Others insist that all the verses of the song should be sung in every case. The issue in contention is the purpose of the song and of all hymns in the worship of the Catholic Church. We are still learning how best to use congregational music.

On the one hand, careful reading of the verses of many hymns makes it obvious that the hymn is meant to be sung in its entirety. The author of the hymn may be telling a story, expressing a theological truth, or offering a prayer. To stop in the middle of this composition makes no more sense than stopping in the middle of the homily (though some would welcome that on occasion, too, no doubt!). An obvious example is singing a hymn to the Trinity but stopping after the verses to the Father and the Son, thus ignoring the Spirit completely! Singing a hymn is not just background for something else. The act of singing is itself both ritual and prayer, and an opening hymn has value even if there is no procession that it accompanies.

On the other hand, the opening hymn usually does accompany a procession, and singing multiple verses long after the procession is over can drag things out unnecessarily. One point to note is that the use of the hymn form at this point is not essential to our ritual. The music used traditionally was a psalm or portion of a psalm. Perhaps we need more music written precisely to accompany this entrance procession instead of using hymns created for other purposes. At the same time, it must be said that the use of hymnody in our worship is common both to various ancient traditions and to the contemporary Protestant tradition as well.

Perhaps one solution to the problem is to look carefully at how we handle the procession itself. Often the procession seems to be carried out on a purely functional basis. Those in the procession move quickly, and often rather carelessly, bunched together so that they almost step on one another's heels. A procession is really a form of simple dance, a choreographed movement. Taking the procession seriously might mean slowing the movement down, beginning only after the first verse is partially or completely sung, leaving ample space between the various ministers, and moving with a measured gracefulness that speaks the importance and prayerful nature of the ritual act. In this way, perhaps the song and the procession will more closely coincide without having to truncate every hymn after two verses.

The Greeting

After the entrance song is finished, the presider leads the assembly in the sign of the cross, followed by a greeting. The sign of the cross was not in the proposed Order of Mass when it was sent to Pope Paul VI, but he felt it should be included. The greetings listed in the Sacramentary are all based in Scripture, and the new Sacramentary will offer five additional options. Some presiders, in an effort to be more personable, have substituted a colloquial greeting like "Good morning" for these biblical texts. While such an attempt is understandable, it manifests a lack of understanding of ritual language and behavior. In the context of worship and prayer, the greetings given, or other biblical formulas, are much more appropriate.

After the greeting, the Sacramentary notes that the "priest, deacon, or other suitable minister may very briefly introduce the Mass of the day." The words "very briefly" are important here; this is not the time for a secondary homily. A few carefully chosen (which means prepared in advance) words are much more effective than a paragraph of rambling thoughts. The introduction here, especially if spoken by the presider or deacon, might lead directly to the penitential rite or water rite.

It should be noted, too, that this is the proper place for introductory comments, not before the opening song. Their place here reminds us that their character should be that of a call to worship, an invitation to enter into the celebration, rather than a didactic explanation of a theme.

The Blessing and Sprinkling of Water

At any Sunday Mass, the penitential rite may be replaced by the blessing and sprinkling of water. This rite is designed as a reminder of baptism, which is the very basis of our assembly. Our identity as the Body of Christ enables us to offer the sacrifice of Christ, and our baptism is the basis of that identity. While the use of this rite is especially appropriate during the fifty days of Easter, it can be used anytime the community would benefit from reaffirming their identity as the baptized people of God. This is also the appropriate time to bless whatever holy water the community needs for its use in worship or at home. There is no need for the priest to bless water in the sacristy. This community sacramental should always be blessed in the presence of the community.

The sprinkling rite after the blessing is meant to bring each member of the assembly into contact with the water. Good use of this ritual requires more than a perfunctory wave of the aspergillum (many parishes use an evergreen branch and a glass bowl for this ritual today) toward the people. Often it will require a bit of time to move down several aisles so that all may feel the water rain upon them, but inclusiveness is important. Very large assemblies may find it best to have the deacon or other ministers assist the presider in this rite. When the sprinkling is extended, it might best be accompanied by a song, perhaps with a congregational refrain and verses sung by the choir or cantor, so that the assembly can focus on the ritual gesture rather than on hymn books.

The Penitential Rite

This part of the Entrance Rites presents the most problems and suffers from the greatest misunderstanding of all the

introductory elements. Much of the confusion is understandable, because the rite itself is a bit confused. Three options are
given in the Sacramentary, and they are quite different in character. Calling them all the penitential rite suggests that they
are very similar, but in fact, they are quite distinct.

The first option, a somewhat revised version of the *Confiteor*
(I confess) followed by the *Kyrie,* is rather obviously penitential in character. The second option, an abbreviated *Kyrie* with
a request for salvation, also admits our guilt ("we have sinned
against you"), and then asks for God's mercy and love. The
third option, a *Kyrie* expanded with tropes, is the form most
commonly used and also the form most commonly misused.

A review of the eight samples of this option included in the
Sacramentary makes it clear that the tropes are intended to
focus our attention on Christ and on his actions on our behalf.
They are not intended to be a recital of our sins. Not one single
example in the twenty-four invocations of Christ mentions our
particular failings. The purpose of the rite is to remind us of
God's mercy and to praise Christ who has achieved our salvation. The revision of the Sacramentary proposed by the
International Commission on English in the Liturgy (ICEL)
lists this litany as a separate option from the penitential rite,
calling it a litany of praise.

This raises a fundamental question about the role of a penitential rite at this point in the Mass. Many liturgists have long
questioned the value of this rite, noting especially the difficulty of shifting moods so quickly. If the assembly has just
sung a rousing and joyful entrance song, it is difficult if not
impossible to quickly shift into a penitential mood and then
return immediately to the joy expressed in the Glory to God.
Even an individual cannot shift gears that rapidly; for a group,
it is simply unrealistic. The result is either a dampening of the
joy appropriate to Sunday or a superficial penitential rite.

ICEL's suggestion that the third option be renamed a litany
of praise points to one possible resolution of the problem of
shifting moods. The cry "Lord, have mercy" is often seen as
specifically penitential, but its history reveals its use as a more
general acclamation of the Lord. It almost has the character of
a cheer rather than a begging for forgiveness. The key to

understanding this may lie in the Hebrew word *hesed,* which means God's steadfast love and mercy. The phrase "Lord, have mercy" is a cry for God's continued covenant love. The focus is not on our sinfulness but on God's love. Thus this litany invokes Christ and focuses on the gift of forgiveness. Awareness of this gift, recognition of the fact that we are all forgiven sinners, can be a strong motive for praise and gratitude that does not clash with the motifs of joy and celebration.

The main focus of the penitential rite, then, at least on most Sundays and major feasts (it may be very different in Lent, for example) is not on our sinfulness and need to repent, but on God's mercy and the gift of divine forgiveness. For the rite to work in practice, however, it is essential that presiders and planners avoid any suggestion that this is time to examine our consciences and confess our sins. Too many people have gotten the impression that this brief rite is a substitute for the sacrament of penance, when its function is actually quite different. Planners who compose their own tropes for the third option (which is a good practice) should take care to ensure that all of them focus our attention on Christ and not on our particular sins. Another help to a more healthy view of this rite would be a modification of the invitation at the beginning of the rite. Instead of saying, "let us call to mind our sins," the presider might use words like "let us call to mind God's great mercy" or "let us rejoice in the gift of forgiveness God has given us in Christ."

Planners should note, too, that all three invocations of this ritual address Christ. In the pre-Vatican II days, many of us learned that the triple *Kyrie* was addressed to the three persons of the Trinity, but the examples in the Sacramentary make it clear that all of these invocations are addressed to Christ.

The Glory to God

The Glory to God, or *Gloria,* as we noted in the last chapter, was often used as an entrance song in the past. Its current use causes some problems on many Sundays through the year. There is little question that its use on major feasts and in seasons of great celebration (i.e., Christmas and Easter) is appropriate. When it is used at these times, it certainly should be sung. It is good for us to spend some time singing this hymn, which is one of the few parts of our worship that is simply extended praise. A number of contemporary settings of this hymn make the assembly's participation easy, with a repeated refrain alternating with verses by a cantor or choir.

The problem comes in Ordinary Time, when singing the Glory to God seems like too much elaboration of the Entrance Rites, but reciting it is deadening. Currently the Glory to God is designated for use on every Sunday except during Lent and Advent. The proposed revision of the Sacramentary makes it one option among the six that may be used between the greeting and the opening prayer, which would allow parishes to omit it when it seems too much to sing it. Until such revisions are approved, planners might sometimes use the Glory to God as the entrance song. A simpler sung setting might also be used on Ordinary Time Sundays as a middle road between a fully exuberant setting and mere recitation.

The Opening Prayer

As ICEL's proposal and the *Directory for Masses with Children* both indicate, the opening prayer is an important part of the Introductory Rites, for it is never omitted. It is the most ancient part of the Entrance Rites, and it deserves more attention than is usually paid to it.

The *General Instruction of the Roman Missal* describes the opening prayer as follows:

> Next the priest invites the people to pray and together with him they observe a brief silence so that they may realize they are in God's presence and may call their petitions to mind. The priest then says the opening prayer, which custom has named the "collect." This expresses the theme of the celebration and the priest's words address a petition to God the Father through Christ in the Holy Spirit.

In practice, the "brief silence" before the collect is often so brief that it is useless. What is clearly intended here is a silence long enough for the assembly to recollect its thoughts and recall the petitions that each brings to this Eucharist. Five seconds is not adequate! It seems to me that we should aim for a silence of a full minute or longer, so that it is a deliberate communal silence. This will require, of course, some education of the assembly as to the real purpose of this silence, and the time should probably be lengthened gradually over a period of weeks so that people can become accustomed to the experience of shared silence as a time of intense prayer. Then the collect will truly have something to collect.

The *General Instruction* also notes that the opening prayer "expresses the theme of the celebration." In fact, the terse character of the traditional Roman collect often fails to fulfill that goal adequately. One of the major additions in ICEL's revision of the Sacramentary will provide new opening prayers based on images drawn from the readings for each of the three lectionary cycles. When these are completed and approved, the opening prayers should do a better job expressing the focus of the day's celebration.

A final consideration with the opening prayer is the question of music. There is much precedent in our tradition for the presider to chant the opening prayer, using a simple chant pattern. Such a practice, at least on major feasts, might well provide the kind of attention to the opening prayer that has been lacking in our recent past. It is a possibility that should not be dismissed lightly.

Conclusion

If our vestibule has been too cluttered lately, we might hope for the day when ICEL's proposed revision receives full approval. Then we can put some of the vestibule's furniture into the closet on certain Sundays and make our entry into worship a bit more simple. In the meantime, we can at least straighten up the vestibule a bit and give prominence to one item in the entrance at a time, letting the others recede into the background that Sunday. Careful planning with judicious restraint can allow the Entrance Rites to fulfill their dual function: to make us aware that we are a community entering into a communal act of worship and to prepare us to hear the Word and celebrate the Eucharist well.

Questions for Reflection and Discussion

1. Does the entrance song in your worship generally help you to recognize the focus of the season or feast being celebrated? Can you name several examples?

2. Is the entrance song normally one that the assembly knows well? How would you rate the level of participation by the assembly in this first element of the liturgy? Does it serve to unify the assembly?

3. How are new songs introduced to your community? Do people have adequate opportunity to learn them before being expected to make them part of their prayer?

4. How many verses of hymns are normally used in your community's worship? Why?

5. What are processions like in your community? Are they things of beauty and prayerfulness or just functional movements? Do the participants "dance" or just "saunter"?

6. How does your presider greet the assembly? Are the scriptural greetings effectively used? Do you find "Good morning" appropriate? Why or why not?

7. Does your community use a "call to worship" after the greeting? Who prepares it? Is it helpful to the assembly? How might it be improved?

8. Is the sprinkling rite used in your community? When? Why or why not? If used, is it an effective reminder of baptism? What might make it more effective?

9. What is your experience of the penitential rite? Is it a reminder of God's merciful love or a recital of our sins? Do you think it fills a needed function at the beginning of Mass? Why or why not?

10. Does your community usually sing the Glory to God when it is used? Do you find it good to take time simply to praise God with this hymn?

11. Is the opening prayer recognized by your assembly as the most important part of the entrance rites? What would help to highlight it? Is adequate silence allowed between "Let us pray" and the text of the collect? Is the prayer spoken slowly enough to register? Is it ever sung?

CHAPTER 5

Encountering the Word of God

I was still in seminary when the missal revised during the pontificate of Paul VI was issued (1969), so my education about the Mass needed some rapid updating. It was a time when all Catholics had to learn rather quickly many new ideas about worship. I still remember my father objecting to the "new Mass," because it took as long to get from the beginning of Mass to the end of the Liturgy of the Word as it did for the rest of the Mass, the "really important parts." Like all Catholics who learned their religion before the Vatican II reforms, we had been taught that there were three important parts of the Mass: the offertory, consecration, and communion. As long as you were present for those three parts (i.e., from the time the priest uncovered the chalice until he received Communion), you had fulfilled your obligation. Attending the earlier parts of the Mass was encouraged, of course, but it wasn't seen as essential to the liturgy.

Unfortunately, that view of the Mass overlooked a major part of the celebration. The *General Instruction of the Roman Missal* says, "The Mass is made up as it were of the liturgy of the word and the liturgy of the eucharist, two parts so closely connected that they form but one single act of worship. For in the Mass the table of God's word and of Christ's body is laid for the people of God to receive from it instruction and food. There are also certain rites to open and conclude the celebration" (#8). This passage reflects the teaching of the Constitution on the Sacred Liturgy of Vatican II, which also speaks of the two main parts of the Mass forming one act of worship and

35

notes that "this Council strongly urges pastors that in their catechesis they insistently teach the faithful to take part in the entire Mass" (#56).

Encounter, Not Classroom

In the years following the council, Catholics have come to recognize the Liturgy of the Word as an integral part of our worship. But it may not be as clear what is supposed to be occurring during this part of the Mass. Many Catholics seem to view the Liturgy of the Word as some kind of Catholic version of Sunday School, a time for Scripture study or for catechesis of the parish. It is often viewed as an educational time, a time to learn more about our faith and the moral implications it should have in our lives. Often Catholics at adult education programs will ask why pastors don't teach the content of such presentations at the homily on Sunday so that the whole parish would hear it. The assumption seems to be that the Liturgy of the Word is a time for adult education.

Many of us began working with the revised Mass under such assumptions. Masses were commonly planned around themes, and Mass planning sheets bore a striking resemblance to classroom lesson plans. Once the point of the Mass was determined, then it was explained in the introduction to the Mass, highlighted with comments before each reading, treated more thoroughly in the homily, prayed about in the intercessions, and summarized one more time in the dismissal comments. We wanted to be very sure that everyone learned the lesson for the day. This approach was especially typical of children's Masses planned by their teachers, but many parish liturgy committees were just as strongly educational in their planning.

A rethinking of the Liturgy of the Word, however, leads us to some very different conclusions. The "Introduction" to the Lectionary for Mass reminds us that "Christ is present in his word; as he carries out the mystery of salvation, he sanctifies us and offers the Father perfect worship. . . . That word constantly proclaimed in the liturgy is always, then, a living, active word through the power of the Holy Spirit. It expresses the Father's love that never fails in its effectiveness toward us" (#4). In the next paragraph, this document insists that "the more profound our understanding of the liturgical celebration, the higher our appreciation of the importance of God's word. Whatever we say of the one, we can in turn say of the other, because each recalls the mystery of Christ and each in its own way causes that mystery to be ever present" (#5).

In this document, as in the Constitution on the Liturgy and in the Sacramentary, a parallel is drawn between the presence of Christ in the word and his presence in the Eucharist. We are fed from two tables: the table of the word and the table of the body of Christ. In both cases, what we should be seeking is not an educational experience but a spiritual one. We seek to encounter Christ, who is the Incarnate Word. In the Liturgy of the Word, Christ speaks to us. In the Liturgy of the Eucharist, Christ offers his body and blood as our food and drink. Both tables are offered for the nourishment of our spirits. Both provide us with the opportunity to encounter Christ and to be transformed by that encounter. Both forms of Christ's presence should give rise to a sense of reverence, for he is really present in the word proclaimed as he is in the bread and wine shared.

The proclamation of the word at Mass, then, is intended to be an opportunity to meet Christ in the word proclaimed. Many Catholics have missed this opportunity simply because they do not expect to find Christ there. Most Catholics still recognize Christ's presence in the bread and wine more quickly than in the word. If we come to the Liturgy of the Word expecting education or Bible study, we are not likely to have the spiritual encounter that is intended.

The Power of the Spoken Word

Much of our problem may actually lie in the way we look at words themselves. We live in an age that is inundated with words. We are constantly being bombarded by words, and we frequently note that "talk is cheap." We may not be very conscious of the power of the spoken word in our culture.

Earlier cultures, more dependent on the spoken word for communication before the advent of printing, were more aware of its power. The Hebrews expressed this, for example, by using the same word *dabar* to mean "word" or "event" or "reality." Speaking a word was an event; it made things happen and changed things. Once spoken, it could not be retrieved. Haven't we all had times when we wished we could take back the word we said? But we can't really; the very speaking of the word causes things to change.

The power of the spoken word is at its greatest when that word is the word of God. God said: "Let there be light," and there was light. That's a powerful word! The word of the Lord compels the prophet to speak, even when the prophet doesn't want to do so. Jeremiah says, "I will not mention him, I will speak in his name no more. But then it becomes like fire burning in my heart, imprisoned in my bones; I grow weary holding it in, I cannot endure it" (Jer 20:9). Through the prophet Isaiah, the Lord says: "For just as from the heavens the rain and snow come down and do not return there till they have watered the earth, making it fertile and fruitful, giving seed to him who sows and bread to him who eats, so shall my word be that goes forth from my mouth; it shall not return to me void, but shall do my will, achieving the end for which I sent it" (Isa 55:10-11). The word of God causes things to happen.

The word of God as an event reaches its fullness with the coming of Christ, the Incarnate Word. "In times past, God spoke in partial and various ways to our ancestors through the prophets; in these last days, he spoke to us through a son," says Hebrews (1:1-2). It is that all-powerful Word that we seek to encounter in the liturgy today. When the word of God is proclaimed to the assembly, Christ speaks to us today, and the words he speaks are words of power. They are meant to change things, to change the hearts and lives of all who hear them. They are not intended to be studied as much as they are to be heard and accepted and lived. Some theologians speak of the proclamation of the word as a kind of sacrament, for it is an event that enables us to encounter Christ and grow in grace.

Listen, Don't Read Along

Understanding the Liturgy of the Word as a sacramental moment to encounter Christ through the word proclaimed has important implications for how this part of the Mass is celebrated. Many parishes rely on missalettes so that people can read along while the word is proclaimed. We got into the habit of reading along when the priest was using Latin and we followed in our missals. When the Mass began to be celebrated in English, we still felt like we should have something in our hands, and missalette publishers have been only too happy to oblige. But reading along and listening attentively are very different activities and often have very different results.

As Marshall McLuhan and others pointed out years ago, the invention of the printing press was linked historically to an increased individualism in our culture. Before printing, for example, there was only one Bible in most towns, often chained to the pulpit since it had to be copied by hand. Access to the Bible was through its proclamation during worship. One of the first books Gutenberg printed on his new printing press was the Bible, and the individual interpretation of Scripture soon gained great prominence with the Protestant Reformation.

When I have my own copy of the text in hand, I am no longer dependent on the proclamation to the community. I am independent. I can read it faster or slower than the lector, I can read it backwards or forwards or upside down if I choose! I am in control of the word. But for a spiritual encounter with the living Word of God in our midst, we need to surrender control, to let God be in control, to submit ourselves to the word. If Christ were physically present in robe and sandals speaking to us at Mass, would any of us dare to (or even want to) follow the text in the book? Yet we believe that Christ is actually present, proclaiming his word through the lector or deacon or priest. We are called to listen, not to read along. And we are called to listen together, for the word of God is addressed to the whole assembly and belongs to the community. It is most properly heard and understood in the context of the church community.

Some biblical scholars and pastors have made the point that reading along while the word is proclaimed is better for learning, since it engages two senses at the same time, which generally fosters more effective learning. I would agree with this position if the purpose of the Liturgy of the Word were Bible study. But if the purpose is a spiritual experience of Christ speaking to us today, then it is better to sit back and listen with open ears and open hearts. Of course, it is very helpful if the listener is familiar with the word before the proclamation. Catholics are increasingly involved in weekly Bible study, which is a healthy sign of growth in the Church. The more we develop a familiarity with the Scriptures, the more we will benefit from the Liturgy of the Word. Bible study that follows the Sunday lectionary is especially useful in preparing for the experience of the liturgy. Since many Catholics are not in Bible study groups, however, many parishes print the citations for the following Sunday's readings in the bulletin each week so that parishioners can read the readings from their Bibles at home in preparation for Sunday Mass. When we come to church already familiar with the readings, we are free to relax and let the Lord speak to us; we may find it easier to hear the word that Christ wants to address to us through all the words of the readings. But even if we are not prepared in advance, it is not important that we catch every word or understand every sentence in every reading. What is important is that we hear the word of the Lord that Christ addresses to us that day. Perhaps on a given Sunday I will be so struck by a line in the first reading that I don't even hear the next two readings or the first half of the homily. So what? If that word of the Lord has touched my heart and leads me to change my life in some way, isn't that enough? It is more than most people seem to get out of the Liturgy of the Word when they approach it as a classroom experience!

Good Acoustics and Lectors

Getting rid of missalettes and learning to actively listen to the word of God would be a great improvement in the Liturgy of the Word in most parishes. But before this step is taken, parishes must make sure that the sound system is adequate for easy hearing and that lectors are thoroughly trained to proclaim the word with life and power. Even then, parishes should make a few copies of missalettes or Sunday missals available (perhaps at the church doors) for those who are hard of hearing and for those who emotionally need to have something in their hands. But that is very different from putting them in all the pews, which implies that the assembly is expected to read along.

A side benefit of moving away from missalettes might also be an increased respect for the word of God, since we will no longer be throwing it in the trash every month! And the money saved over two or three years will enable the parish to pay for good hymnals, which is a much better music resource for parish worship than the limited and temporary selection provided in missalettes.

Some parishes also indicate a heightened respect for the word of God by keeping the Lectionary enthroned in the church, sometimes with a candle near it to parallel the candle used near the tabernacle. This simple but powerful symbol can remind everyone that Christ is present in the word as well as in the bread.

Putting aside our own texts also reminds us that the Liturgy of the Word is a communal event, not a private one. We can and should read the Scriptures on our own every day, but when we gather in worship, we listen to the word of God together. In fact, when lectors are well-trained and proclaim the word with power, most people will spontaneously put down the text and listen. They recognize that something important is happening in the proclamation itself and instinctively know that the communication is enhanced by looking at the person speaking to them. Personal communication is much more than words; eye contact, facial expressions and posture contribute to the experience, as does rate of speech, tone, and expressiveness on the part of the proclaimer. The proclamation of the word is an event shared by all those present. In the next chapter, we will examine the various parts of the Liturgy of the Word to see how we can make it more of an event for the assembly.

The liturgy is a powerful teacher, which forms us in the knowledge and love of God and of God's Son and of the Holy Spirit. But it does not teach as a classroom teacher does. It forms and shapes our attitudes and our lives more power-fully and more subtly. We find ourselves changing and grow-ing in faith to the extent that we truly encounter Christ in the Mass. Both at the table of the word and at the table of the bread, we are invited to recognize the presence of the Incarnate Word. Then we are called to open our ears, our mouths, and our hearts to let him transform us more and more completely.

Questions for Reflection and Discussion

1. How important do you think the Liturgy of the Word is to the members of your assembly? Is it recognized as parallel to the Liturgy of the Eucharist or is it seen as preliminary to the "important parts" of the Mass?

2. What image seems to be dominant in your community's approach to the Liturgy of the Word? Is it seen as an educational opportunity, a time for Bible study, or is it clearly an opportu-nity for a spiritual encounter with the living Christ? What fac-tors suggest which image is dominant?

3. Are your community Masses planned around a theme? If so, is the theme really organically drawn from the readings, the feast, or the season, or is it imposed on the liturgy?

4. Do you feel that you are being well fed from the "Table of the Word" as well as from the "Table of the Bread"? If this is more true on some days than others, what makes the difference?

5. Does your assembly recognize the presence of Christ in the word proclaimed? What makes you answer as you did?

6. Do the lectors in your community proclaim the word with power? What about the deacon or presider? What kind of training is offered for proclaimers of the word?

7. Do most people in your assembly listen attentively to the word proclaimed or do they read along? Have they been taught

the importance of active listening? Is the text of the readings in every pew, encouraging reading instead of listening?

8. Is Bible study encouraged in your community? Are there Bible study groups? Are materials made available to encourage personal reading of the Scriptures? Are the readings for next Sunday listed in each week's bulletin so that people can prepare for Mass at home?

9. Is the sound system in your church truly adequate? What steps can be taken to improve it?

10. Is the Liturgy of the Word in your community experienced as an "event," a time to encounter Christ, a moment of great significance? What can be done to heighten the assembly's awareness of the proper meaning and power of this experience?

CHAPTER 6

Letting Loose the Power of God's Word

"What do you remember from the readings this morning?" the mother almost asked the children on the way home from church. Then she suddenly realized that she couldn't remember what they were about either! She had been there for the whole Liturgy of the Word and had tried to listen carefully, but even before she reached their home, it had all vanished from her mind.

Unfortunately, her experience is not that unusual. Sunday after Sunday, millions of Catholics gather for Mass, hear the word of God proclaimed, and leave Mass largely unchanged by the experience. Often parishioners will blame this fact on the poor quality of preaching in many Catholic churches. Yet if the word of God is truly a powerful word, a word that could create the universe from nothing, then its very proclamation should have an effect on us, whether or not the homily that follows is well done. Why do we keep missing the power of God's word?

A major part of the problem lies in our expectations. There is so much misunderstanding about the purpose of the Liturgy of the Word that many Catholics do not expect anything of great significance to happen during that part of the Mass. Since we are most often anticipating some kind of educational experience (Sunday school or Bible study), we are not prepared and often not even open to the kind of spiritual experience that hearing the word of God proclaimed can offer. There is a great need to help Catholics come to understand the Liturgy of the Word as a time to encounter Christ as he speaks to us today, a time to come in contact with the all-powerful word of God that created the universe and can re-create us. An openness to the power of that word is the first prerequisite for making the Liturgy of the Word all that it can be for us.

Training Lectors

The second most important step we can take to bring this part of the Mass to life is to have well-trained and practiced lectors who can proclaim the word with all the power that it bears. When we first began to use lectors after Vatican II, the need was immediate and there was not much time for training. Sometimes the only criterion for choosing lectors was whether they could read English! In the intervening years, most parishes have recognized the need for some kind of lector training days or programs, and the quality of lectors has certainly improved over the past quarter-century.

The problem that remains here is often one of expectations, too. Lectors (and sometimes their trainers) often think that their job is to read from a book. The very word "lector" is Latin for "reader." We would be taking a step in the right direction, however, if we translated it "proclaimer." The task is not just to read words on a page, but to proclaim to the assembled people of God the good news of revelation. This requires much more of the proclaimer than simply reading words.

What is supposed to happen in the Liturgy of the Word is vital human communication. One person, the proclaimer, has something important to communicate to all those listening. And communication with a large group is an art that requires the development of skills which many people in our culture do not possess without training and practice. Some of these are simply the basic skills of public speaking, while others involve knowing the word of God and how to share it.

For example, when we really want others to hear something we wish to tell them, we naturally make eye contact when we are speaking to them. We all know how disconcerting it is to have someone speaking to us who avoids looking us in the eye. The lector must learn to speak the word of God while making eye contact. This skill is just the opposite of what most of us do instinctively. We look down while we read and look up when we pause. What we need to do is look down at the pauses to get the next phrase or sentence and then look at the assembly while we speak the words. Other basic speaking skills involve rate of speech, enunciation, and effective use of the microphone. These skills need to be practiced until they become second nature for the lector.

Beyond public speaking skills, the lector also needs to acquire a solid knowledge of the word of God and of the purpose of the Liturgy of the Word. Many lectors, like many of their hearers, have a great hesitation about proclaiming the word with power. We have been taught to be reserved and reverent in church, and many feel that this excludes the use of dramatic expression in the proclamation of the word. Some worry about seeming to be too dramatic or theatrical. But what is needed here is not "hamming it up" or phony emotionalism. What is needed is simply a conversational style. We need to bring to the proclamation of the word the same range of vocal ability we use in normal conversation with friends and family. When we speak with others, we are usually quite animated, especially if we care about what we are saying. We speak loud and soft, fast and slow, with pauses and emphasis, with facial expressions and full eye contact. The problem is that in church we speak abnormally, in reserved tones and with flat expression that ends up depriving the proclamation of the word of the power that it contains. The result is boredom in church and readings quickly forgotten after Mass.

Obviously, to proclaim the word with its power intact also requires that the lector clearly understand the meaning of the passage. This requires basic Bible study as well as regular use of commentaries on the Scriptures as part of the preparation for the Sunday readings. It also requires sufficient time to reflect upon the readings and pray over them so that their meaning in the lector's own life becomes clear before he or she attempts to share that message with others.

It should be apparent at this point that the ministry of lectors requires much of both the lector and the parish. The lector must be willing to take time for thorough training and then to prepare carefully each time he or she is scheduled to proclaim the word of God. The parish needs to invest adequate time and money to provide the extensive training that will enable lectors to fulfill this ministry effectively. There are various lector training programs available in most areas, but the first step is to recognize that an evening or two is generally not sufficient. After years of training lectors, I have found that seven to ten sessions are a minimum for developing the skills needed and overcoming the inhibitions that keep lectors from becoming true proclaimers of the word.

Celebrating the Word As If It Mattered

Committing the time and money necessary to develop excellent lectors is a clear indication that the parish considers the Liturgy of the Word important. The way this part of the Mass is actually celebrated should also reflect its importance. One of the most basic issues is the time we allow for the word to be heard and savored.

After the opening prayer is completed, the assembly is seated and the lector approaches the ambo. The lector should pause significantly before beginning the proclamation. It takes time for everyone to get seated and settled, to be ready to really hear what is to come. During this time, the lector should establish eye contact all around the assembly. If some people begin to wonder why the reading has not started, that simply means they will be more attentive when the proclamation begins.

The Sacramentary notes that after each reading and after the homily, silence should be observed so that all can "meditate briefly on what has been heard" (#23). This is a very important element in the Liturgy of the Word, but it is often omitted or observed so briefly as to be useless. What is needed here is a lengthy shared silence to allow the word to sink in and take root. If a parish has had no silence after the readings, it might be best to begin with only about fifteen seconds, but this time should be gradually lengthened until a full minute (or even two!) becomes normal and comfortable.

After the silence, the responsorial psalm is sung. Though the Sacramentary allows the psalm to be recited, it is clear that the proper function of the psalm is a sung response to the proclaimed word. There is a rhythm and alternation between reading and song throughout this part of the Mass. Reading the psalm and/or the Gospel acclamation violates that pattern and diminishes the power of the liturgy. Singing the psalm is not as difficult as some parishes seem to think. There are numerous collections of psalm settings available today that offer ease of congregational response with a bit more complex and beautiful verses for the choir or cantor to sing. If singing the assigned psalm each Sunday seems too ambitious at first, choose one of the seasonal psalms (Lectionary, #175—in the revised Lectionary, #174) and use it for several weeks in a row. After a few years of regularly singing these psalms and gradually adding new ones to the parish repertoire, the assembly may be able to sing more and more of the assigned psalms as they occur.

The second reading should also be framed with silence, a brief moment at the beginning and a longer reflective time after. Then all stand for the Gospel acclamation and procession. The *Alleluia* (or its Lenten substitutes) should always be sung. To recite it is as effective as reciting the Happy Birthday song at a party. The *General Instruction* even notes that if it is not sung, it may be omitted (#39). The revised "Introduction" to the Lectionary is even stronger, saying that it "must be sung" (#23). The *Alleluia* and Gospel acclamation should be a strong musical piece that truly acclaims the Lord present in the Gospel about to be proclaimed. The acclamation is to accompany the Gospel procession. In too many parishes, the priest or deacon waits until the acclamation is finished before moving to the ambo to proclaim the Gospel. The movement might wait until the first *Alleluia* is repeated; then the deacon asks the blessing or the priest bows before the altar while the verse is sung, moving from the altar to the ambo during the final *Alleluia*. At least on some occasions, the Gospel procession should be more elaborate. Servers might accompany the priest or deacon with candles and stand on each side of the ambo during the proclamation. Incense might be used to show our reverence for Christ in the word. A special Gospel book may be placed on the altar at the beginning of Mass and solemnly carried to the ambo during the acclamation. And sometimes the book might even be carried through part of the assembly for a longer procession. All of this will express in symbol and ritual the importance we place on the word of God and especially on the Gospel.

The Pastoral Introduction prepared for the new Sacramentary also suggests that the gospel might be sung, or at least the greeting, the title, and "The Gospel of the Lord," with the assembly singing their responses. On solemn occasions, the *Alleluia* might be repeated *after* the people's response at the end.

The Homily

After the Gospel is proclaimed, silence is also appropriate, though in some parishes the homily begins immediately with a longer silence for reflection before the profession of faith. The homily itself, of course, is an important element in the Liturgy of the Word. It is intended to bridge the gap between the era when these readings were written and our own time. The homily should generally be based on one or more of the readings just proclaimed, though the *General Instruction* notes that it may develop "another text from the Ordinary or the Mass of the day" (#41).

Much has been written in recent years about the type of preaching that is properly called a homily. Without getting involved in all the technicalities of preaching types, we should note that a homily is neither mere exegesis of the Scripture (Bible study) nor moralistic preaching ("you should or should not do . . ."). The homily should attempt to do just what the Scriptures do, which is mainly to proclaim the good news of God's actions on our behalf. The homily should generally lead the assembly to gratitude for what God has done and continues to do in our midst; then the assembly will be ready to enter into the great act of thanksgiving that we call Eucharist.

Those who deal with the day-to-day needs of parish life will likely argue that it is often necessary to use the homily time to address other matters. At this point in history, most adult Catholics do not accept their responsibility to continue their education through adult education, Catholic reading, etc. So sometimes it is necessary to instruct the assembly on some issue or another, maybe even on the meaning of a part of the Mass itself. Sometimes there are crucial moral or social issues that need to be addressed. Sometimes there are financial needs that must be brought to the assembly's attention. Trying to make the homily really be a proclamation of good news every week often runs head on into these concerns.

I would suggest two basic principles that should guide pastoral decisions on preaching. One is that a clear majority of the preaching in a parish should be truly homiletic, truly proclaiming the good news. Exceptions to the rule should be exceptions and not become the rule. The second principle is that even these other needs must be clearly linked to the readings and/or the feast being celebrated. This might mean waiting a few weeks until the readings provide a basis for raising the issue involved. And even in these cases, the preacher should strive to lead the assembly to gratitude for God's love and gifts. This is the best basis for asking people to respond to God, whether by changing behavior, donating money, or volunteering time. The whole of our life in Christ should be a response to God's goodness to us. Motivating people by guilt or by logic is generally less effective than inviting a response based on gratitude. When we feel blessed and loved, we are more likely to be generous with our time and money and effort.

We Will Be Changed

All these elements of the Liturgy of the Word are meant to help the assembly truly hear the word of God and take it to heart. When this word is clearly proclaimed and attentively heard, then its power is set loose in our midst. No one who truly hears God's word can remain unchanged by the experience. And no assembly that takes the Liturgy of the Word seriously will remain the same week after week. Sometimes dramatically, more often slowly but steadily, they will be shaped by God's word into an ever more effective image of Christ, so that they can live more clearly as his Body in the world today.

Take some time to evaluate the Liturgy of the Word in your parish. Consider what could be improved to make this part of the Mass more clearly a time for encountering the Lord present in your midst. The time invested in careful evaluation and improvement will reap valuable dividends in the spiritual growth of the parish.

Questions for Reflection and Discussion

1. How many lectors does your community have? How many of them proclaim the word powerfully and effectively?

2. What kind of training has been offered to those willing to serve in the ministry of the lector? Is it required or just an option for those interested?

3. Do your lectors make and maintain eye contact with the assembly? If some do, do you find this disconcerting or helpful?

4. Can you think of a time recently when the word really came alive for you as it was proclaimed? What fostered that experience?

5. Have you ever heard a lector who seemed to be "hamming it up"? Can you express the difference between that approach and a truly powerful proclamation of the word?

6. What kind of study materials are made available to the lectors in your community? Does each lector have one or more commentaries on the Scripture or a workbook with the year's readings and proclamation suggestions? Are materials available in the sacristy or parish library for those who want to study further?

7. Is the Liturgy of the Word in your community celebrated with care and a reflective style and pacing? Would it be evident even to a passerby that something important is happening?

8. Is silence maintained after the first and second reading and after the homily? How long? Should it be longer?

9. Is the responsorial psalm sung at every Mass, at least on Sundays and holy days? What steps are necessary to reach that standard?

10. Is the Gospel acclamation always sung? Does it accompany the Gospel procession? Is the procession extended on special days or during the festal seasons?

11. How would you evaluate the preaching in your community? What makes a homily effective for you? How could you help those who preach to be even more effective?

12. Does the proclamation of the word of God have an effect in your community? Can you name ways in which you or the assembly as a whole have been changed by it? What would make the experience more powerful for your assembly?

CHAPTER 7

The Hinge of the Mass

"What are the principal parts of the Mass?" the speaker asked the adult education group. Though a few still remembered when the offertory, consecration and communion were considered the three principal parts, most of the group had learned since Vatican II to speak of the Liturgy of the Word and the Liturgy of the Eucharist as the two main divisions of the Eucharist. "And at what point do we move from the Liturgy of the Word to the Liturgy of the Eucharist?" the speaker continued. That's when confusion erupted. Many in the group considered the homily to be the final part of the Liturgy of the Word, but others noted that the preparation of the gifts began the Liturgy of the Eucharist. So what about the Profession of Faith and the Prayer of the Faithful—where do they belong?

The confusion is understandable. The official books list these two elements as part of the Liturgy of the Word, yet the catechumens, who participate in the Liturgy of the Word, are dismissed before the creed. After the proclamation of the word and the homily, there is to be a period of silence for reflection before the creed, which makes these two elements seem like a new section. They are a response to the word of God, just as the whole Liturgy of the Eucharist can be viewed as a response to the word. Yet they are not really part of the meal portion of the Mass, the Liturgy of the Eucharist. They really function as a kind of hinge between the two major parts of the Eucharist, leading us from the word to the table.

The Creed

In early Christian worship, the Profession of Faith was connected primarily with the celebration of baptism. The triple immersion in the baptismal waters was preceded by a triple profession of faith in the Father, the Son and the Holy Spirit. In the fifth and sixth centuries a profession of faith was added to the Mass in many areas, though it was not included at Rome until the eleventh century. The Creed used at Mass is often called the Nicene Creed, because it began its life at the Council of Nicaea (325), though the form we use was modified by the Council of Constantinople (381) and ratified by the Council of Chalcedon (451).

The *Directory for Masses with Children* suggests using the Apostles' Creed when the assembly is mostly children, "especially because it is part of their catechetical formation" (#49). The new universal catechism issued in English during 1994 also uses the Apostles' Creed as the outline for its presentation of the basic beliefs of the church. The U.S. bishops recently approved a proposal to make the Apostles' Creed an official option at all Masses, either recited whole or divided into parts as in the renewal of baptismal promises at Easter. They also approved a slight change in the translation of the Nicene formula, which removes the exclusively male reference ("for us men and for our salvation" becomes "for us and our salvation"). These changes, if approved by Rome, will be part of the new Sacramentary, which should be forthcoming soon.

Effective use of either formula of the profession of faith during Mass is a challenge. The length of the text and its complex sentences make recitation difficult and often muddled, yet singing the text seems to put too much emphasis on it, again because of its length. Several pastoral adaptations may help keep the Creed fresh and vital for our assemblies. Some parishes use the baptismal promises, with their question and answer format, throughout the whole fifty days of Easter; this might help us remember the link between the Creed and baptism and recognize that each time we profess our faith, we are renewing our baptismal commitment. A similar format, using the Nicene formula, could also be used on occasion. On solemn feasts, the Creed might be sung, perhaps using a simple chant or using a repeated refrain for the assembly's participation. Such variations can help all to be attentive even when the Creed is simply recited together. A few words of introduction to the Creed, spoken by the presider, can also increase awareness, such as: "Let us join together now to profess the faith we share with Christians around the world" or "As baptized members of the Body of Christ, we are proud to profess our faith before the world."

The General Intercessions

The Prayer of the Faithful or General Intercessions are a unique part of the Mass. Though the format and general categories are standard, the actual text of these prayers is intended to be unique to each worshiping assembly each time it gathers. This is the primary place where the current experience and needs of the assembly are to be integrated into the worship.

Unfortunately, many assemblies are deprived of the richness that this prayer can offer, because no one invests the effort needed to create good current prayers. Too many parishes use printed samples of the General Intercessions straight from the book. Many of these were written years ago, and even those which are in periodical materials still must be written months in advance of the date they are used. There is thus often nothing current or local about these general intercessions.

What is supposed to happen is that each parish community writes its own Prayer of the Faithful for each day. Printed examples can be valuable resources from which to mine ideas and even phrasing at times, but the prayer must be tailored to the concerns of the local community and the events of the day. Anything less defeats the whole purpose of including this prayer in the midst of our worship.

This means, of course, that each parish will need to find and recruit those members of the community who have a gift for poetry. The prayers are not rhyming poems, of course, but they should be composed in a poetic style, which is to say that they should rely more on concrete images than on abstract ideas. It is much better, for example, to pray "that we may cherish the green canopy of the trees, the blue depth of the sky, and the crystal clear water of the stream" than to pray "that we may be ecologically aware and committed to the environmental movement." A poetic writer draws on concrete images to express abstract ideas.

Categories of Petitions

The *General Instruction of the Roman Missal* lists four general topics that should regularly be included in the General Intercessions: "As a rule the sequence of intentions is to be: a) for the needs of the Church; b) for public authorities and the salvation of the world; c) for those oppressed by any need; d) for the local community" (#46). This list provides a helpful framework in composing petitions. Within each category, there may be one or several petitions, but all four categories should be included normally, though the *General Instruction* adds that "in particular celebrations, such as confirmations, marriages, funerals, etc., the series of intercessions may refer more specifically to the occasion." Even on those occasions, however, it is good to include the four categories to keep our prayer from becoming too narrow.

There is a balance needed in the General Intercessions between local and universal concerns. While current events and local needs should be included, this is the prayer of the whole assembly and should also link us to the larger Church. Thus we may pray for members of the parish who are hospitalized, but we should also include all who are sick. We might pray for our pastor and parish ministers, but should also pray for church leaders around the world. In other words, the prayer should speak the concerns of the local assembly, but the assembly should be concerned with the needs of all. In this prayer, the faithful exercise their responsibility to intercede on behalf of all people as Christ gave his life for the salvation of all.

One danger in composing petitions is the temptation to use the prayer as a way to push a particular view or political position. Planners should regularly critique the petitions to be sure that they are prayers we can legitimately expect the whole assembly to embrace. The petitions must be true prayer, not a way of challenging those who disagree with us.

Structure of the Prayer

Those who compose the General Intercessions should be clear about the structure of this prayer. It begins with an introduction spoken by the presider inviting the assembly to enter into the prayer. The petitions are then voiced by the deacon or another minister. Then the prayer is concluded with a collect prayer spoken by the presider. The opening introduction is an invitation to prayer; it is addressed to the assembly, not to God. The final collect is a prayer and thus is addressed to God.

The petitions themselves are a mixture in their normal format. The actual words of the petition are really addressed to the assembly, inviting them to pray for a particular intention. The assembly's response is the actual prayer. The assembly is invited ". . . let us pray to the Lord," and the actual prayer is "Lord, hear our prayer." Thus the petition itself is not addressed to God (e.g. "Grant your comfort to those who grieve") but to the assembly. One easy way to evaluate a petition on this score is to reverse the structure and see if it makes sense to say "Let us pray to the Lord that. . . ." Generally, too, this prayer follows the general pattern of prayer in the liturgy, which is to say that it is addressed to the Father, through Christ, in the Spirit, rather than being addressed to Christ.

It should be noted that there are exceptions to this general rule. Sometimes in the Liturgy of the Hours and within the celebration of the sacraments, the ritual includes intercessions that are addressed to Christ rather than the Father, and sometimes the petitions themselves are addressed to God or Christ rather than being invitations to the assembly. But the normal pattern for Sunday Eucharist is the pattern described above.

Those who compose the petitions each week need to be closely attuned to the local community as well as informed about national and world events. It is helpful to have several people involved in the composition process, even though one author should be assigned the writing task on a given week. A planning group can suggest issues of concern and people who need the community's prayer, thus helping the one composing the prayer to avoid too narrow a perspective. Many parishes also have a book in the vestibule in which parishioners can list people and needs for which they ask the community's support in prayer. Such a book can suggest topics for the intercessions, especially if a given concern (e.g. unemployment, children leaving the Church, political oppression) appears several times.

One way to highlight the General Intercessions is to set them to music. A good cantor can chant the petitions to a common pattern with a little preparation, thus leading the assembly into a sung response, or the petitions can be read with soft instrumental background leading into the assembly's sung response. The addition of music can do much to create a more prayerful context for the petitions.

Even when the petitions are spoken, there are ways to foster a more prayerful mood. A significant pause after each petition allows the assembly to focus more fully on each request. A short pause might also be placed just before the final phrase of each petition—"let us pray to the Lord" or "we pray to the Lord." This would allow the assembly to embrace the intention before they make their spoken or sung response.

Conclusion

These two hinge elements of the liturgy are brief but important parts of our worship. With careful preparation and prayerful use, they can serve well as the assembly's response to the word of God they have just heard proclaimed and, at the same time, lead the assembly into the Liturgy of the Eucharist which follows. For parish poets to shape prayers that speak from our hearts to the heart of God, let us pray to the Lord!

Questions for Reflection and Discussion

1. What is your experience of the proclamation of the Creed at Mass? Is it prayerful? Does it truly express your own faith? Have you ever sung it? Do you prefer singing or reciting it? Why?

2. Is the renewal of baptismal promises at Easter a powerful experience for you? Why or why not? Would it be good to use this form of professing our faith more often?

3. Who composes the petitions for the Prayer of the Faithful in your assembly? Are they well written, with concrete images and gracious language? Who do you know that might have a gift for such writing?

4. Do the petitions each week reflect current issues and local community concerns? How can the true concerns and needs of the assembly be regularly included?

5. Are the four main categories of petitions included each week? Is there adequate variety in the particular concerns in each category?

6. Is there a good balance between particular local concerns and universal needs?

7. Are the petitions ever sung in your community? Is the response sometimes sung even when the petitions are recited?

8. Are the General Intercessions prayed slowly enough and with appropriate pauses? Are they experienced as a strong moment of prayer by the whole assembly?

9. Does your community recognize and embrace its responsibility to intercede for others and for the whole world? Do members of the assembly see this as a way of identifying with Christ, who gave his life for others? How could such awareness be heightened?

CHAPTER 8

The Offertory That Isn't

When the revised Missal was issued in 1969, astute observers quickly noted that the section of the Mass that had been called the Offertory no longer appeared under that title, but was now called the Preparation of the Gifts. This shift of names was a deliberate change which indicated a change in the understanding of this part of the Mass. As Fr. (later Archbishop) Annibale Bugnini, the Pope's spokesman at the time, had written earlier, "This sector of the celebration, not touched on in previous reforms, is now to be reordered so that it will correspond better with its true meaning" (*L'Osservatore Romano*, May 22, 1968).

What, then, is the "true meaning" of this section of the Mass? If it is not an offertory, why had it been known by that name for so long? A bit of history can be enlightening. The prayers that were used in this part of the Mass before Vatican II were not ancient; they were first used in Rome in the fourteenth century and only fixed in the Roman Missal in 1570. What is more ancient and more fundamental to this part of the Eucharist is bringing the gifts forward. As early as the third-century, we find a formal presentation of the gifts to the bishop and a blessing of the gifts. In addition to the bread and wine needed for the Mass, it was customary to bring forward other things that were needed for the support of the church and for the poor.

The title "offertory" apparently stemmed from this ritual act. "To bring forward," in Latin, is *ob fero*, which eventually was combined into one word, *offero*. The song which accompanied the bringing up of the gifts was called the *offertorium*, which became (inaccurately) offertory in English, which suggested an offering of a sacrifice rather than the bringing up of the gifts. The new Missal thus changed the name to Preparation of the Gifts to better reflect "its true meaning."

Theology of Sacrifice

This shift in name has important theological implications. For centuries, Catholics and Protestants have disagreed about the sacrificial nature of the Mass. As the reformers insisted, following the Letter to the Hebrews, there is only one sacrifice in the New Testament, the sacrifice of Christ. No other sacrifice is acceptable or necessary. Yet the Catholic Church has long called the Mass a sacrifice, and many Catholics spoke of this part of the Mass as the time when the bread and wine was offered to God. We were even encouraged to spiritually place ourselves on the paten as the priest lifted it up to God. This led to the unfortunate impression that the Mass was a sacrifice somehow distinct from the self-sacrifice of Christ.

In fact, the Mass is a sacrifice to the extent that it is a sharing in the one sacrifice of Christ. Christ's sacrifice of himself is both historical and eternal. It was historically expressed in his death on Calvary and resurrection from the tomb. But Jesus is "forever victim, forever priest," because the core of his sacrifice is his submission of his will to the Father's, and that act is an eternal act. He is forever in perfect union with the Father's will, and we can share in his sacrifice if we also submit ourselves to God's will as he did.

This one eternal sacrifice, in which we share in the Eucharist, is Jesus offering himself to God. There is no other sacrifice in the New Testament. We do not offer bread and wine or anything else to God except the sacrifice of Jesus. We offer ourselves to the extent that we are conformed to Christ, being his Body and sharing his act of submission to the Father. As the Second Eucharistic Prayer for Reconciliation puts it, "we ask you, Father, to accept us, together with your Son." To call the Mass a sacrifice is not to claim it as a sacrifice separate from the one redeeming sacrifice of Christ but to recognize it as the way we share in that one sacrifice.

Practical Implications

This theology also has practical implications for both liturgy planning and personal spirituality. This part of the Mass is a time of preparation, both for the gifts and for the assembly. This is the time the assembly prepares to enter into the great Eucharistic Prayer and the Communion which follow. The gifts are brought forward and the altar is prepared. At the same time, the assembly should be preparing spiritually to enter fully into the Eucharistic Prayer and Communion, preparing themselves to share the sacrifice of Christ by making his attitude their own.

The history of this rite reminds us that it is the procession with the gifts that is the core ritual. The most ancient and most basic of the prayers is the Prayer over the Gifts after they have been placed on the altar. This ritual and prayer mark the "setting aside" of the bread and wine for the Eucharistic meal that follows. Many parishes have found it difficult to get volunteers to bring up the gifts at each Mass; perhaps this indicates a lack of understanding of this rite as a time to express the assembly's willingness to enter into the meaning of the Mass, the sacrifice of Christ.

The procession with the gifts should be carried out with sufficient focus and reverence to suggest its importance. The gifts should be carried from the back to the deacon or presider before or at the altar. The primary gifts to be carried forward are the bread and wine; these ought to be of the finest quality and should be sufficient to provide for the communion of all present. Under ordinary circumstances, all the bread and wine that will be used during a given Mass should be presented by representatives of the assembly. Communion should not come from the tabernacle, except by way of exception. All the bread and wine used is included in the procession; there should not be separate portions of bread and wine on the credence table.

Along with the bread and wine, it is proper to bring forward the monetary offerings of the assembly, along with any other "gifts to meet the needs of the church and of the poor" (*General Instruction*, #101). These gifts are not put on the altar, but should be placed in a suitable spot nearby; the collection should not be removed for counting until after the Mass is finished. The linking of the collection (called the offering in some churches) with this part of the Mass might lead some to think that this is an offertory, but a better understanding perceives the donations of the people as a symbol of their willingness to enter into the sacrifice of Christ which is offered during the Eucharistic Prayer.

It is not appropriate to include in the procession with the gifts any other items, either practical or symbolic. The water, the chalice, a purificator, and other items needed for the Eucharistic meal are brought to the altar from the credence table, generally while the collection is being gathered. On some occasions, members of the assembly might prepare the altar itself, bringing the altar cloth, candles, flowers, book, etc., before the procession with the gifts. The practice at children's Masses of bringing textbooks, footballs, and other symbols of the children's lives distorts this ritual. If such items are desired as part of the worship environment, they should be put in place before Mass or perhaps included in the entrance procession, which is also an appropriate time at a funeral to bring forward items symbolic of the life of the deceased. A good rule of thumb for what is appropriate in the procession with the gifts is that whatever is brought forward is not returned to the owners after Mass; it is either used for the meal or given to the poor or the church.

Spoken and Silent Prayers

In the context of the whole Mass, the preparation of the gifts is not a major section. It is relatively simple and functions as a kind of pause between the intensity of the Liturgy of the Word and the solemnity of the Eucharistic Prayer. A hymn may be sung, especially to accompany the procession, but this may also be a good time for instrumental music or a choir motet or for prayerful silence. If a hymn is used, it should not speak of offering but of preparing, or it may be a song of praise or a seasonal hymn. Any song used at this point should be called the Preparation Song or Presentation Song rather than the Offertory Song.

The only prayer that must be said aloud is the Prayer over the Gifts, including the call to prayer—"Pray, my brothers and sisters . . . ." The proposed new Sacramentary has an option to use the simple "Let us pray" as the call to prayer. There are also two blessings that may be said aloud by the presider, and the people may respond with "Blessed be God forever." These may also be said silently, as they should be whenever singing or music is part of the preparation. All the other prayers are private prayers of the priest (or deacon) and should never be said aloud; the rubrics note that these texts are said "inaudibly."

Ritual Actions

The U.S. bishops have voted to allow the option of enacting the sign of peace at the beginning of the preparation of the gifts, preceded by a brief invitation reminding us of Jesus' words that we should be reconciled before we bring our gifts to the altar. If that decision is approved by Rome as part of the new Sacramentary, this optional addition will take its place as part of the assembly's preparation for entering into communion with Christ and with one another.

The primary ritual action in this part of the Mass is the bringing up of the gifts and then placing the bread and wine on the altar. In contrast to the older missal, the current Sacramentary says the priest holds the bread and then the cup "slightly raised above the altar." This is not a gesture of offering but one of setting aside. The elevation of the bread and wine comes at the Great Amen of the Eucharistic Prayer.

The presider should be the one who places the bread and cup on the altar. When the gifts are presented, the presider might receive the money and the wine first, handing them to acolytes. Receiving the bread last, he carries it to the altar and places it in the center. The cup is prepared at the side of the altar and then placed in the center. If a deacon receives the gifts and prepares the cup, the bread might be placed on the side of the altar while the cup is prepared either at the altar or at the credence table (*General Instruction*, #133). Then he hands the bread and the cup to the presider who places them in the center of the altar. The blessing prayers (silently or aloud) should accompany this action of placing the gifts on the altar; there is no need to place the gifts and then pick them up again for the prayers.

If incense is used, the incensation of the gifts and the altar is followed by the incensation of the presider and the assembly. This symbolizes the uniting of the assembly with the gifts that will be used in the sacrificial meal. After the incensation, the presider washes his hands. Though this originally may have been a practical necessity after receiving gifts of meat and produce, it soon became a symbolic action of spiritual purification. The prayer is said inaudibly, so the symbol should be rich enough to speak on its own. Use a pitcher, bowl and towel, not a cruet, tray and napkin. And teach the acolytes to pour a significant quantity of water, not just a few drops.

Evaluating Parish Practice

Presiders and liturgy planners should evaluate the parish's patterns of song, word and action during the Preparation of the Gifts. Such an evaluation will indicate what improvements can be made so that it lives up to its name and its purpose of preparing the altar, the gifts, and the people for the Eucharistic Prayer and Communion.

Questions for Reflection and Discussion

1. Is the Preparation of the Gifts clearly secondary to the Liturgy of the Word and the Eucharistic Prayer? What do people in your community call this part of the Mass? What term is used for the song during the preparation?

2. Do you think most people still think of this as a time of offering a sacrifice to God? Do you understand the ecumenical issue this raises? How can we help Catholics recognize that there is only one sacrifice in the new covenant? Could you

explain to others in your community how we are to enter into the one sacrifice of Jesus?

3. Is this part of the Mass well-utilized as a time to prepare to enter into the Eucharistic Prayer, sharing in Christ's sacrificial act of worship? How might the assembly be led to appreciate this time as a preparatory moment?

4. Does your community make use of the procession with the gifts at each Mass? Is it carried out with beauty and grace? How are people recruited for this procession? Is the composition of the community reflected in the variety of those who present the gifts?

5. Are the bread and wine used the best quality we can provide? Is the bread able to be recognized as real bread and large enough to be broken and shared among the faithful? Could the bread be baked by members of the assembly each week? Are the vessels for the bread and wine beautiful and well maintained?

6. Is all the bread and wine to be used at the Mass presented in the procession? Is enough bread consecrated for each Mass or is communion regularly distributed from the tabernacle?

7. Is the collection taken up with grace and dignity, and is the money handled with reverence as the people's gift? Is the money included in the procession with the bread and wine? Are other items included, too? Are they appropriate? Why or why not?

8. What is heard during the Preparation of Gifts—song, silence, spoken prayers, assembly responses? Are the silent prayers said silently? How often is it appropriate to say the blessing prayers aloud? What do you find most helpful in preparing for what is to come?

9. Are the gifts "placed" by the presider rather than elevated? Is incense ever used at this part of the Mass?

10. Is the washing of the hands done with a beautiful pitcher and bowl and a real towel? If not, why not?

11. Is the prayer over the gifts proclaimed with prayerful dignity? Could it be sung on solemn feasts?

CHAPTER 9

The Core of the Mass

The Eucharistic Prayer presents a difficult pastoral challenge to those who prepare the liturgy. It is clear theologically that this great prayer of thanksgiving is the core of the whole Eucharist, its most important part. Yet it is hard to make it clearly important experientially.

There are a number of reasons for this pastoral difficulty. One is the contemporary penchant for variety, to which the liturgy responds at various points. The Liturgy of the Word offers us different readings every week over a three-year cycle. The repertoire of music available in most parishes provides a large number of hymns and psalm settings, so that the same songs need not be used too frequently. The prayer of the faithful invites different petitions each week, as the needs and concerns of the community change. All the collect prayers of the Mass change each week, and the new Sacramentary promises even more alternatives than we currently have.

By contrast, the Eucharistic Prayer is relatively unchanging. Before Vatican II, of course, it was completely unchanging, except for the preface and a few festal inserts. We had only one Eucharistic Prayer, the Roman Canon, whose title—canon—indicated its unchanging nature. Now we have four standard prayers, plus three for children, two for reconciliation, and one for Masses for Various Needs and Occasions. Yet even this number does not compare to the variety of the other texts of the Mass. The words soon become familiar if not routine.

Another reason for the pastoral difficulty is the nature of the prayer as an extended proclamation by the presider. The

Eucharist has no other text this long proclaimed by one person (except the homily!), and members of the assembly may find it difficult to stay tuned in. The ritual attempts to respond to this difficulty by integrating sung responses by the assembly. The four standard prayers and the two for reconciliation have three responses: the "Holy, Holy," Memorial Acclamation, and Great Amen. The prayers for children add other acclamations to these, creating a more dialogic style of prayer, and many authors have suggested that the other prayers should also have more frequent acclamations for the assembly. The prayer for various needs and occasions has additional optional acclamations when the whole prayer is sung.

A third factor in many parishes is a general lack of understanding of the nature and structure of the Eucharistic Prayer. Without such understanding, the prayer may well seem like a random sequence of sentences rather than an integrated poetic whole.

A fourth issue may simply be the fundamental nature of the prayer itself. The Eucharistic Prayer is primarily a prayer of praise and thanksgiving. Such a prayer will have great significance for those who are conscious of how much they have received from God and are therefore filled with gratitude. But that type of faith seems uncommon among Catholics today. We seem much more aware of our own needs and wants than we are of what God has given us, so we find prayer of petition more in tune with our attitude than an extended prayer of praise and thanksgiving.

Jewish Roots of the Eucharistic Prayers

Before considering some pastoral suggestions for better use of the Eucharistic Prayers, it may be helpful to look at their relatives. The Christian Eucharistic Prayers seem to be related to Jewish prayer forms. Over the past several decades there has been ongoing historical debate about the specific Jewish prayer form that gave rise to the Christian Eucharistic Prayers. Some scholars have focused on the *berakah*, a blessing prayer that blesses God for the good things God has done. Others favor the *hodayah*, which is a prayer of thanksgiving. It is similar to the *berakah,* but thanks God rather than praising God. Several scholars see the origins of the Eucharistic Prayers in the Jewish meal prayer called *Birkat ha-Mazon,* which seems to be composed of a *berakah* and a *hodayah.*

The precision that scholars seek is not critical for our understanding of the Eucharistic Prayer. All of the Jewish prayer forms mentioned have a similar dynamic. The prayer blesses or thanks God, recalls God's marvelous deeds and favors, asks God to favor us today as in the past, and concludes with a final word of praise or blessing.

It seems that this basic pattern of prayer was common among the Jewish people in biblical times, and various examples can be found in the Scriptures. Some of these examples seem very spontaneous and others seem more formal. The spontaneous blessing or thanksgiving has a brief expression of blessing or thanking God and then an expression of the reason for which God is being praised or thanked. In Genesis 24:26-27, for example, Abraham's servant blesses God for helping him to find a proper wife for Isaac. (See Exod 18:9-10, Luke 10:21, and Matt 11:25-26 for some other examples.)

The more formal prayer begins the same way, though the reason given for the prayer is a more extended recital of God's wondrous deeds, often covering much of salvation history. This recalling of God's wondrous deeds leads to petition that God's mercy will continue in the present and the future. The prayer then concludes with another blessing or doxology. Some examples of such extended prayers may be discerned in Psalm 103 and 104 and Ephesians 1:3–3:21.

This general type of prayer would probably have formed the main prayer at the Last Supper, as at all Jewish meals. If the Last Supper was actually the Passover supper, the recital of God's wondrous works would no doubt have been more elaborate than on other days. The early Christians continued to meet for religious meals after the resurrection, presumably including what God had accomplished through Jesus in their recital of God's wondrous works. Gradually prayers would have developed with a more clearly Christian content and language.

Current Eucharistic Prayers

Our current Eucharistic Prayers reflect this ancient Jewish prayer forms. The structure is perhaps easiest to see in the fourth Eucharistic Prayer, but it can be discerned in each of the others. We begin each prayer with a standard formula that calls the assembly to enter into praise and thanksgiving: "Let us give thanks to the Lord our God. It is right to give him thanks and praise." After the initial praise we recall various wonders God has done, ranging from creation to covenant to the prophets to the death and resurrection of Jesus. Included in this recital of saving acts of God is the narrative of the Last Supper. Awareness of God's goodness leads naturally to petitions for God's continued help. The first petition is always for the unity of the Church through the power of the Holy Spirit, the fundamental purpose of the Eucharistic meal. Then we pray for church leaders, for the living and the dead, and that we might all one day share the life of the saints who have gone before us. The prayer always concludes with a standard blessing of God, the doxology that leads to the Great Amen.

The basic structure of the prayer (praise and thanks, recital of God's deeds, petition, doxology) also determines the placement of the three standard acclamations by the assembly. The Holy, Holy is primarily a communal expression of praise linked to the opening blessing of God. The Memorial Acclamation focuses on the greatest of God's saving acts, the death and resurrection of Christ. The petitions do not have a separate acclamation but are concluded by the final doxology. With the Great Amen the assembly responds to the final doxology and thus affirms the whole meaning of the prayer.

Anamnesis and *Epiclesis*

Within this basic structure of the prayer, we can also note several important elements. Two of them are designated by Greek words, *anamnesis* and *epiclesis*. English lacks a good equivalent to translate *anamnesis*, which means more than "remembrance" or "memorial." It is the name given to the whole recalling of God's wondrous deeds in the Eucharistic Prayer, though it applies particularly to the remembrance of the death and resurrection of Jesus, which is expressed clearly in the prayer just after the Last Supper narrative (e.g., in the third Eucharistic Prayer: "Father, calling to mind the death your Son endured for our salvation, his glorious resurrection and ascension into heaven . . ."). This same part of the Eucharistic Prayer generally expresses most clearly the offering of the sacrifice of Christ: e.g., ". . . we offer you in thanksgiving this holy and living sacrifice."

Just after the *anamnesis*, the prayer moves to the *epiclesis*, which is the invoking of the Holy Spirit. The first petition prays for the unity of the Church as a result of the presence of the Spirit: e.g., "Grant that we, who are nourished with his body and blood, may be filled with his Holy Spirit, and become one body, one spirit in Christ." In the Roman tradition of Eucharistic Prayers, there is also commonly an *epiclesis* before the Last Supper narrative, invoking the power of the Holy Spirit over the bread and wine that they will be transformed into the body and blood of Christ: e.g., "We ask you to make them holy by the power of your Spirit, that they may become the body and blood of your Son, our Lord Jesus Christ. . . ."

The Institution Narrative

One of the most important shifts needed for many Catholics to understand the Eucharistic Prayer revolves around the Last Supper narrative or institution narrative. Because it recalls the historical basis of the Eucharist itself, this part of the recalling of God's wondrous works has naturally become central in our awareness. The problem comes when we think of this narrative as a kind of magical moment of consecration, viewing the recital of the words of Jesus as a magical formula that "brings Christ down upon the altar."

We know that Christ is present already in our midst through the assembly, the priest, and the word proclaimed, so it is not a matter of Christ coming where he was not. We do believe, however, that the bread and wine are truly changed into body and blood of Christ, and the Eucharistic Prayer is the context of that transformation. In the effort to determine precisely the moment of consecration, the Western Church focused on the words of Christ, while the Eastern Church focused on the *epiclesis,* the prayer invoking the power of the Spirit. The debate continued for centuries, and both positions have merit: the words of Christ speak the identity of the bread and wine transformed, but this occurs only through the power of the Spirit at work in the Church. Rather than choosing one moment over the other, most theologians today speak of the whole Eucharistic Prayer as consecratory. The prayer is an integral act of praise and thanks to God proclaimed over the bread and wine, which are thus consecrated and transformed into the body and blood of Christ. This perspective puts the institution narrative in its proper context, seeing it as part of the great prayer rather than as magical words.

Questions for Reflection and Discussion

1. Does the Eucharistic Prayer seem to you to be the most important part of the Mass? Why or why not?

2. Do you think additional acclamations throughout the Eucharistic Prayer would be helpful?

3. How can the assembly be educated about the nature and structure of the Eucharistic Prayer? Do you think this would help them enter more fully into the prayer?

4. Are you usually aware of the blessings of the past week as you arrive for Mass? Does gratitude for God's gifts shape your attitude regularly? How do you think most of the members of your assembly would answer these questions?

5. Does knowing about Jewish prayer forms help you to appreciate the Eucharistic Prayer? Why or why not?

6. Do you see the Last Supper narrative as part of the recalling of God's wondrous deeds or as a quasi-magical moment? How do you think most of your community would answer?

7. Does it make sense to you to consider the whole Eucharistic Prayer as consecratory rather than isolating particular words? Why or why not?

CHAPTER 10

Praying the Eucharistic Prayer Well

In the last chapter we looked at the history, structure, and components of the central prayer of the Mass, the Eucharistic Prayer. This chapter focuses on a variety of pastoral strategies that can make this great prayer of praise and thanksgiving better understood and appreciated by the worshiping assembly. Then we will consider the various prayers that are available today and see how they can best be used throughout the course of the year.

Education of the Assembly

Some of the most important steps for heightening appreciation of the Eucharistic Prayer involve education of the assembly. Every Christian should have some understanding of the background of this great prayer of thanksgiving. Though discussion of the Jewish *berakah* and *hodayah* may seem a bit esoteric to some, knowing the rich history of the Eucharistic Prayer helps today's worshippers connect to a long tradition of prayer and praise. Such education helps the contemporary assembly unite itself with the prayer that Jesus himself would have proclaimed at the Last Supper. It also helps them to understand the richness of the prayer itself and recognize its nature as an extended proclamation of praise and thanksgiving.

The pastoral introduction prepared for the new Sacramentary suggests that the presider might briefly suggest particular motives for thanksgiving before the preface dialogue.

This might also help the assembly to enter more fully into this prayer of thanks and praise.

Another helpful strategy for deepening appreciation of this prayer is to teach people to use the *berakah* form of prayer on a regular basis. This can offer a powerful aid to developing a rich spirituality in everyday life. I have been told that Ortho-dox Jews are expected to recite at least one hundred such prayers every day. Can you imagine the attitude of gratitude such a practice would nurture? Upon waking in the morning, one says, "Blessed are you, O God, for you have given us an-other day of life." Getting out of bed, one might add, "Blessed are you, Lord of all, for legs and feet that still work." Turning on the shower, one could pray, "Blessed are you, Creator of the universe, for you have given us water to cleanse and refresh us." And so, throughout the day, we would find dozens of opportunities to thank God for the countless gifts that we enjoy every day of our lives.

Such a practice of prayer takes no extra time out of our busy schedules, but it brings every moment of the day into a prayerful awareness of God's presence and generosity. This would, in turn, make us so aware of God's gifts that we might truly become a people of thanksgiving, a people who would then be ready to join together on Sunday to praise and thank God in the great Eucharistic Prayer. This is a prayerful way to "count one's blessings," to be aware of all the ways that God has blessed us in the past and continues to bless us each day.

The Jewish form of prayer also provides a simple frame-work for spontaneous prayer before meals in the family. Whoever leads the prayer can begin with a simple expression of praise and thanks to God (e.g., "We give you thanks and praise, Lord our God, creator of all good things . . .") and then add one or several current reasons for this praise and thanks-giving, including the gift of the food about to be shared. Other family members or guests at the table might be invited to add reasons for thanksgiving as well; children readily learn to pray in this fashion. Then the leader can conclude with a simple doxology (e.g., "For all these reasons, O Lord, we praise your holy name, now and forever."). Teaching families to pray in this fashion would provide an alternative to the standard memorized "Bless us, O Lord, and these thy gifts . . . ," and the educational effort might lead many families to begin a practice of prayer before meals that is lacking in many Catholic homes today. This would also provide a basis for deeper appreciation of the Eucharistic Prayer as the Church's prayer before the sacred meal we call communion.

Acclamations for the Assembly

One of the problems with using the Eucharistic Prayer that we noted is that it is an extended proclamation by the presider, the longest element of the Mass that is proclaimed by one person, except for the homily. Some parishes have attempted to overcome this problem by having the whole assembly recite the prayer with the presider, but that does violence to the nature of the prayer and the role of the presider. Our ritual books and the longer tradition of the Church rely instead on sung acclamations for the assembly to ratify what the presider proclaims.

Many commentators have suggested that we need more acclamations than the standard three currently included in all our Eucharistic Prayers. The prayers for children are examples of how such additional acclamations can make the prayer more dialogic in style. These additional acclamations were provided in light of the short attention span of children, but many argue that adults would also benefit from more frequent acclamations throughout the prayer. The Eucharistic Prayer for Masses for Various Needs and Occasions takes a step in that direction, adding an optional acclamation before and after the first *epiclesis* and another one that is sung three, four, or five times as part of the intercessory section of the prayer. These acclamations are used only when the whole prayer is sung. Perhaps future liturgical books will provide other prayers with additional acclamations.

In the meantime, it is important to use well the acclamations that we have. The first and most basic point is that they should *always* be sung. Every Eucharist, especially on Sundays and feasts, should include singing. Even at daily Mass, if a musician is not available, the assembly can still sing the acclamations for the Eucharistic Prayer, thus adding dignity and solemnity to this central part of the Mass.

It is important pastorally, then, that these acclamations be well known and able to be sung easily by the assembly. This does not mean that the parish should always use the same musical setting, but it does mean that whatever settings are chosen should be used frequently enough to be learned by heart by the assembly. It is also very helpful to use consistent "sets" of acclamations, so that the Holy, Holy, the Memorial Acclamation, and the Great Amen are from the same setting or at least similar in style. If the parish has learned several separate acclamations that are not part of full settings, musicians should create their own sets, using the same three acclamations together rather than combining them randomly. This will aid the assembly in responding enthusiastically during the Eucharistic Prayer as well as in singing without accompaniment when that is necessary.

Using the Variety We Have

One of the problems with using the Eucharistic Prayer is the limited variety of prayers currently approved for use. Compared to other variable parts of the Mass, the choices are few. Yet it must be said that the practice in most parishes is even more limited than it need be. Some assemblies never hear anything except the second Eucharistic Prayer, because it is the shortest. Others hear the second and third, with occasional use of the first on major solemnities. Even the regular use of the four basic prayers would be an improvement in many situations. The three prayers designed for Masses with children, the two prayers for reconciliation, and the prayer for various needs and occasions offer further alternatives.

Planners and presiders should choose and prepare the Eucharistic Prayer as carefully as any other variable part of the Mass. Each prayer has its own characteristics and nuances, which may make one more appropriate than another for a given celebration. Each prayer has its own emphases, which may reflect the readings of the day or the focus of the feast. Sometimes phrases from one of the prayers will even appear in the readings, since much of the wording of the Eucharistic Prayers is based on the Scriptures.

In choosing the Eucharistic Prayer, some of the following points may be helpful. The first prayer, the old Roman Canon, does not have its own preface, so it is often useful on major feasts that have unique prefaces. This prayer also has inserts for several major solemnities, which might prompt its use each year on those days. Liturgical books in several other countries offer similar inserts for the second and third prayer, and the proposed Sacramentary contains such texts for certain feasts and seasons and for ritual Masses (baptism, marriage, etc.), but for now only the first prayer offers this feature. This prayer also includes the names of the apostles and other early saints, which might prompt its use on their feasts or when the readings speak of them.

The second Eucharistic Prayer, based on the third-century *Apostolic Tradition* of Hippolytus, is the shortest. It has its own proper preface, although other prefaces may be substituted. Since there is very little of salvation history in the prayer after the preface, any other preface substituted should be as rich as its proper preface. This prayer may be best used on weekdays, with its own preface. It also expresses quite clearly the link between sacramental communion and the unity of the church.

The third Eucharistic Prayer does not have its own preface, so it is often appropriate when there is a proper preface and the first prayer is not used. This prayer also seems especially appropriate when there is a focus on the Holy Spirit (mentioned often in this text) or on the worldwide nature of the Church (". . . from east to west . . ."). Since it makes provision for including the name of the saint of the day or the patron of the parish, it is often the best choice on a saint's feast or a parish anniversary.

The fourth Eucharistic Prayer is the most clearly scriptural, recounting salvation history more thoroughly than the other prayers. Thus it might be especially appropriate when the readings include a passage from the historical books of the Bible, when the prophets are mentioned, or when the covenant is highlighted. It is also appropriate when the mission of Jesus or his concern for the poor is highlighted in the Mass. Other emphases in this prayer are on our call to mission (". . . that we might live no longer for ourselves but for him . . ."), our unity in Christ (". . . gather all who share this meal into the one body of Christ, a living sacrifice of praise."), and the universal scope of salvation (". . . those here present and all your people and all who seek you with a sincere heart."). This prayer is so rich and poetic that it deserves to be used more frequently. The new Sacramentary should resolve the problem of non-inclusive language in the prayer.

The three prayers for children are intended to be used in Masses when the majority of the participants are children. The first of these uses parts of the Holy, Holy for three acclamations by the assembly. This prayer stresses creation as God's gift and the ministry of Jesus which expresses God's love. The second prayer uses several different acclamations, which makes it a challenge musically, but a number of good settings of these texts are available. This prayer stresses God's will that we love one another. The third prayer uses one additional acclamation, repeated several times in the second half of the prayer. This prayer reflects Jesus' mission of reconciliation, bringing people together. It also has special inserts for the Easter season; inserts for other seasons are supposed to be prepared and approved by national bishops' conferences, but none have appeared for the United States so far.

The prayers for reconciliation were created for the Holy Year in 1975 but were intended to be used after that year "when the mystery of reconciliation is a special theme of the celebration." The first of these prayers seems stronger concerning the need for personal repentance and renewal, while the second text is stronger on reconciliation and peace between groups and nations.

Our newest Eucharistic Prayer is to be used with any of the Mass texts found in the Sacramentary under the heading "Masses and Prayers for Various Needs and Occasions." It has four prefaces and four sets of intercessions for different occasions. This prayer is not intended to be used on Sundays or days when ritual Masses are prohibited (see #330 in the

General Instruction) but may be used on many weekdays. The very existence of this Eucharistic Prayer may prompt presiders to consider anew the value of these prayer formularies for various needs and occasions as part of parish life.

Conclusion

Presiders should regularly challenge themselves on their style of proclaiming the Eucharistic Prayer. It is easy to slip into a mechanical recitation, especially with the prayers we use most often. Assemblies recognize immediately when the prayer is proclaimed with care and personal prayerfulness. Every presider should seek to proclaim the prayer in such a way that members of the assembly will sense that "he really means what he is praying."

The pastoral introduction to the new Sacramentary suggests several times that the nature and importance of the Eucharistic Prayer is enhanced when the prayer is sung, especially on more solemn occasions. If the whole prayer is not sung, singing the preface and its dialogue is encouraged.

Despite the limited number of prayers available at this time, the Eucharistic Prayers we have provide a rich treasury of image, theology, and poetry. Careful selection among the prayers and among the eighty-four variable prefaces in the Sacramentary (and even more in the new Sacramentary) will open this treasury more fully to the members of the parish. The Eucharistic Prayer is the core of the whole Mass; its careful selection and proclamation are essential to good worship.

Questions for Reflection and Discussion

1. Would you find daily use of the *berakah* form of prayer a helpful part of your own spiritual life? What else might help you increase your sense of gratitude for God's gifts?

2. Do you (and your family) pray before meals on a regular basis? What form of prayer do you use? Would using the *berakah/hodayah* style help link the Eucharist to your family meals?

3. How could the parish staff or the worship commission help people to develop habits of family prayer that would better link liturgy and life?

4. Are the Eucharistic acclamations always sung in your community? Even for weekday Masses? If not, why not?

5. Were you aware that we have ten approved Eucharistic Prayers? How often are the different prayers used in your community? Who has the responsibility of choosing this central text? Is it part of the liturgy planning process or is it just left to the presider? How can more balanced use of these options be fostered?

6. Which of the Eucharistic Prayers do you like the best? Why? Have you ever used these texts as a basis for your personal prayer and meditation?

CHAPTER 11

Preparing for Communion

While the Eucharistic Prayer is the central core of the whole Mass, it can be argued that the climax of the Eucharist is the sharing in the Body and Blood of the Lord that we call Communion. In the earliest centuries, it seems that Communion followed the Eucharistic Prayer directly, with only the necessary breaking of the bread intervening. At least by the fifth century, however, the Lord's Prayer and a sign of peace had been added as preparatory rites for Communion itself. The introduction of the Lamb of God to accompany the breaking of the bread is attributed to Pope Sergius I at the end of the seventh century.

In subsequent eras, various other elements were added to the preparation for Communion, including various prayers for the priest and for the people, some of which were originally designed for Communion outside of Mass (e.g., the *Confiteor*). Much of this material was removed in the reforms after Vatican II, though some remnants remain. The primary elements of the preparation for Communion today are the Lord's Prayer, the sign of peace, and the breaking of the bread.

The Lord's Prayer

The Lord's Prayer has long been used in all Christian liturgical traditions as the "table prayer" for the Eucharistic meal. Its request for daily bread, though it may certainly include all that we need from God for life, naturally brings to mind the bread of the Eucharist. Its request for forgiveness by

God as we forgive others also fits well the traditional under-standing of Communion as uniting all those who share in the meal in a unity of peace and love in Christ.

The final petition of the prayer has customarily been expanded with a request known as the embolism (from a Greek word meaning "insertion"). This addition, which may be as old as the use of the Lord's Prayer in the Eucharist, repeats the prayer to be preserved from evil and granted peace. Our current rite adds the words, ". . . as we wait in joyful hope for the coming of our Savior, Jesus Christ," which leads smoothly into the acclamation "For the kingdom, the power, and the glory are yours, now and forever." This acclamation, often called the Protestant ending, is really an ancient doxology added to the Lord's Prayer as early as the second century, perhaps to avoid ending with the words about evil. The Byzantine tradition has long concluded the Lord's Prayer with this acclamation, and our recent reforms have introduced it into the Roman rite.

Though earlier practice in the Roman rite assigned the Lord's Prayer to the priest, with the people adding an *Amen* at the end, our current ritual calls for this prayer to be said or sung by the whole assembly. Since we all share a common adoption through baptism, it is appropriate that we pray to our common Father together. This means that it is never appro-priate for the Lord's Prayer to be taken over by a soloist or a choir in order to perform an elaborate sung version. If the prayer is sung, it is to be sung by all.

Singing the Lord's Prayer raises some pastoral difficulties, however. One problem is that singing the prayer tends to overshadow the Eucharistic Prayer, which is more important and thus should be highlighted musically. Singing the Lord's Prayer, the Lamb of God, and perhaps even some music during the sign of peace clearly puts too much emphasis on these preparatory elements. Another challenge is to maintain partici-pation in this prayer if it is sung. Other than perhaps the second chant tone, there does not seem to be any music for this text that is universally known, so singing it often precludes full participation, at least for visitors. A number of settings that were popular a few years ago really did violence to the text itself, using rhythmic patterns that did not follow the pattern of the words in English and often changing the common text. Many also had no provision for the embolism and/or the final acclamation. Such settings are inappropriate for the Eucharist; if the prayer is sung, the embolism and acclamation should be sung as well. Most often, however, it is probably best to recite the Lord's Prayer reverently together.

The United States bishops have approved a rubric for the new Sacramentary that the people may extend their hands in the traditional gesture of communal prayer (the *orans* position) while saying or singing the Lord's Prayer.

The Sign of Peace

Though many Catholics still think of the sign of peace as a recent innovation, a ritual kiss of peace is as old as the New Testament and was part of the Mass from the earliest centuries. In many traditions, it was placed at the end of the Liturgy of the Word, so that the peace was exchanged before the gifts were brought to the altar. The United States bishops have approved this as an option in the new Sacramentary. But as early as the time of St. Augustine (354–430) in Africa, it was placed after the Lord's Prayer, and it was moved to this position in the Roman rite sometime before the fifth century. This position links the ritual with the petition in the Lord's Prayer for mutual forgiveness and thus links it with the whole meaning of Communion itself.

The ritual took various forms through the centuries and gradually was limited to the clergy and eventually only practiced during a solemn Mass. The reforms of Vatican II restored this ritual as an integral part of the Communion Rite. Some confusion has arisen over the rubric, "Then the deacon (or the priest) may add: Let us offer each other the sign of peace." This does not mean that the sign of peace itself is optional, but that the verbal invitation may be spoken or omitted. In many parishes, it is not necessary to tell people to exchange the peace; after the assembly responds to the presider's wish of peace to them, they spontaneously share Christ's peace with those around them.

In the Middle Ages, it was common for the peace to be exchanged first between the presider and his assistants, who then extended it to the assembly. The current rite, however, does not envision the peace as originating with the presider but as arising from Christ who dwells in each member of the assembly. Thus it is not appropriate for the priest to travel the length of the church to extend the peace to each pew or to each person; the rubrics note that "All make an appropriate sign of peace, according to local custom. The priest gives the sign of peace to the deacon or minister." The United States bishops left the particular form of this ritual to develop locally. Most Catholics exchange a handshake, though some embrace or share a kiss. While it seems natural for spouses to share a kiss rather than a handshake, it may not be good ritual to treat some members of the assembly differently than the rest. This ritual sharing of peace is meant to express our unity in Christ, not the distinctions among us. Pastoral prudence may suggest not making an issue of the point, but when the question is raised, a ritual gesture that we can share with all around us seems best.

The other pastoral question that often arises about the sign of peace is its length. In some communities, this ritual lasts longer than Communion itself, as each member of the assembly seeks to greet every other person present. In small group Masses such inclusiveness may be appropriate, but in the normal Sunday assembly it seems excessive. The sign of peace is a ritual action that is part of the preparation for Communion. It should not overshadow the Communion itself, so it should be relatively brief. Another distortion is to make this a time for "chit chat" among community members; hospitality and friendliness are important, but they should be expressed as the assembly gathers for worship. When that happens, the impulse to expand the sign of peace diminishes.

The issue here is really a proper understanding of the purpose of this ritual. Some parishes have moved the sign of peace to the beginning of Mass, so that people will greet one another as the Eucharist begins instead of waiting until Communion time. While the intention is laudable, such revamping indicates a misunderstanding of the sign of peace. It is not a greeting of strangers, but a ritual prayer for Christ's peace to fill the lives of those with whom we are about to share the Lord's Body and Blood. It expresses the meaning of the communion we share in Christ, and it presumes that the assembly has already been hospitable toward one another and toward visitors as people gathered for worship. A proper understanding of this ritual will also help members of the assembly to see it as an integral part of preparing for Communion, not an interruption.

If the bishops' decision is ratified by Rome, the new Sacramentary will allow us to enact this ritual either as part of the Communion Rite or as part of the Preparation of the Gifts. While strong arguments can be raised for either position, it would be unfortunate if the sign of peace were moved from its present place simply to avoid interruption in preparing for Communion. This would support a view of Communion as a private experience that does not involve those around me, which is not at all what Communion is supposed to be. If I am not willing to recognize and unite with all those who share in this meal, then I am not ready to receive the Body and Blood of the Lord. As Paul insisted in 1 Corinthians (11:29), if we eat and drink the Body and Blood of the Lord without recognizing the body (i.e., church), we eat and drink a judgment on ourselves. Parish leaders should discern carefully whether moving the sign of peace to the Preparation of the Gifts would encourage this false understanding of the meaning of Communion.

Even though we have been using this ritual for nearly thirty years now, it is still good pastoral practice to remind parishioners periodically of the meaning of the rite. This might sometimes be part of the homily, especially when the readings focus our attention on the meaning of Eucharist. It might sometimes be an item in the bulletin. And it might occasionally be part of the invitation to share the peace: "As we prepare to enter into communion with Christ and one another, let us express our willingness to be one by sharing a sign of Christ's peace."

The Breaking of the Bread

In apostolic times, this ritual action was so significant that it gave its name to the whole Eucharistic action: "They devoted themselves to the apostles' instruction and the communal life, to the breaking of bread and the prayers" (Acts 2:42). Besides its practical necessity before the age of precut hosts, this action signifies the unity of the assembly who shares the one bread and the one cup. The ancient usage leads us to speak of the "breaking of bread," though the action also includes the pouring of the Blood of Christ into several cups when several are needed for Communion.

This action is accompanied by the singing of the Lamb of God, a text which reminds us that Christ's body was broken and his Blood poured out for our sake. The song and the action are meant to go together and be coterminous. Thus, the breaking of the bread should not begin until the sign of peace is completed and the assembly's attention returns to the altar. The Lamb of God begins at the same time and continues until all the bread is broken and the cups poured. If this takes longer than the usual three invocations, they may be repeated or tropes can be added to expand the litany (e.g., "Lamb of God, living bread come down from heaven, have mercy on us"). Several excellent musical settings incorporating such tropes are available.

One of the reasons that the breaking of bread seems insignificant in many parishes is that the bread to be broken is so minimal. Precut wafers with a presider's host that is broken in half or four pieces are a very inadequate symbol of the one bread we share. The *General Instruction of the Roman Missal* is very clear about the bread that should be used: "The nature of the sign demands that the material for the eucharistic celebration truly have the appearance of food. Accordingly, even though unleavened and baked in the traditional shape, the eucharistic bread should be made in such a way that in a Mass with a congregation the priest is able actually to break the host into parts and distribute them to at least some of the faithful. . . . The action of the breaking of the bread, the simple term for the Eucharist in apostolic times, will more clearly bring out the force and meaning of the sign of the unity of all in the one bread and of their charity, since the one bread is being distributed among the members of one family" (#283).

Ideally, the bread should be baked by members of the parish each week. Various recipes are available for unleavened bread, and organizing a ministry of baking bread can be another way to help parishioners take ownership of the liturgy. If commercial hosts are used, at least some of the bread should be large enough to be broken into many pieces, and the action should be done in a visible and reverent gesture for all to see. There is no need for a separate host for the clergy; we all share the one bread.

Before the Lamb of God, there should be only one container of bread and one cup of wine on the altar, if possible. This presumes large vessels if the assembly is large. In such cases, a carafe of wine might be needed in addition to the chalice, though large chalices (with a suitable lip for pouring) are available that will hold enough wine for most assemblies. The bread and the wine are both divided during the Lamb of God. All the bread and wine used for a given Mass should be consecrated at that Mass; distributing from the tabernacle should be clearly an exception, when unexpected numbers cause a shortage at distribution or when too much bread has accumulated in the tabernacle and needs to be used. In these exceptional situations, the reserved sacrament is brought unobtrusively to the altar during the Lamb of God. This is also the appropriate time for ministers of Communion to come from the assembly to the altar and for any additional cups and plates to be brought to the altar from the credence table. The deacon and/or some of the Communion ministers may help with the dividing of the bread and wine for distribution.

Conclusion

These three rituals form an integral movement from the Eucharistic Prayer to Communion. All three speak of our oneness in Christ and lead us to enter more deeply into union with Christ and with all the members of his Body. Prayerful and reverent use of these elements can do much to create a true experience of the sacredness of Christ's presence in his Body and Blood.

Questions for Reflection and Discussion

1. Which part of the Mass seems more central to you: the Eucharistic Prayer or Communion? Why?

2. What part of the preparation for Communion do you find most helpful personally? How does it help you enter more fully into Communion?

3. Does your community normally sing or recite the Lord's Prayer? What advantages do you see to each option?

4. Where do you think is the best place for the sign of peace? Do you experience it as an appropriate part of preparing for Communion? Why or why not?

5. What gesture and what words seem the best choice for the sign of peace? Is a simple handshake adequate? What variations have you experienced?

6. Does your community use bread that can be broken and shared among many members of the assembly? Is the breaking of the bread a significant ritual action, done so that all can see it? Does the Lamb of God accompany the breaking of the bread and the pouring of the wine until all is prepared?

7. Could your parish bake its own unleavened bread? Is this central symbol of our worship important enough to warrant the effort needed to organize such a ministry?

8. Are there only one container of bread and one (or two) vessels for wine on the altar before the Lamb of God? If not, why not?

9. Is all the bread and wine needed for a given Mass normally consecrated at that Mass? Is there any need to bring bread from the tabernacle at most Masses?

10. Do you think most members of your assembly recognize the communal dimensions of Communion, or is it primarily a private moment with Jesus? How can we come to a fuller appreciation of what it means to be one body as we share in the one bread and one cup?

CHAPTER 12

Sharing the Body and Blood of the Lord

In my current ministry I have the opportunity to preside at Eucharist at many different parishes, filling in for priests who are ill or on vacation. The experience is sometimes encouraging and sometimes disheartening, but it is always interesting, for I get to experience how various communities celebrate. One of the most disconcerting aspects of this ministry is finding parishes who do not offer the assembly the opportunity to share both the Body and the Blood of Christ.

Many reasons are given when I ask why Communion under both species is not common practice at all Masses. Sometimes the problem is a lack of adequate ministers, sometimes the priest who usually presides at that Mass doesn't want to do it, sometimes the people seem unwilling to share the cup, and sometimes it is just a matter of saving money by not having to buy so much wine!

What is disconcerting to me as a presider is to stand before the assembly and proclaim Christ's words in the Eucharistic Prayer, "Take this, all of you, and drink from it; this is the cup of my blood," while I know that I am not able to offer it to them. It seems to be such a contradiction at the heart of the Mass. It seems obvious that Christ intended us all to share both his Body and his Blood. Depriving the assembly of that opportunity is hard to justify.

Communion Under Both Species

The Second Vatican Council decreed the restoration of Communion under both kinds, and subsequent decrees gradually expanded the occasions when it could be offered. At this point in the United States, Communion under both species can be offered at every parish Mass on Sundays and on weekdays. The only exception would be situations with such large numbers (e.g., a papal Mass outdoors, perhaps) that distribution could not be managed reasonably.

If your parish does not share both the Body and Blood of the Lord at all Masses, moving to that standard is the most important step you can take to improve the Communion Rite. The full use of symbols is a basic principle of the renewal of the liturgy. This also implies, of course, the best bread and the best wine that we can provide. The bread should look and taste like real bread and be able to be broken and shared. The wine should be good wine, which does not necessarily mean a wine that only connoisseurs can afford. It should be a wine that most of the assembly finds pleasing, which usually means a middle ground, not too sweet and not too dry. To choose the wine based solely on the taste preferences of the presider is to suggest that the Mass really belongs to the priest, not to the whole Church. For symbolic purposes, a red wine (or at least rose,) is better than white for suggesting the Blood of Christ; it is also more clearly visible in a glass carafe or cup.

A Banquet, Not Leftovers

A second step in improving the Communion Rite is to clearly use the symbols of bread and wine as the food and drink for a sacred meal. When you have guests over to your house for dinner, you do not generally serve some people freshly prepared food while others are given leftovers. So, too, at the Eucharist, the standard is that all the bread and wine used at a given Mass should be consecrated at that Mass. Distribution of bread from the tabernacle should clearly be the exception rather than the norm.

For many years, I thought that this principle was a part of the reforms after Vatican II. I learned later (from the newsletter of the Federation of Diocesan Liturgical Commissions, May–June, 1993) that it dates from just after the Council of Trent. An encyclical of Pope Benedict XIV in 1591 and the encyclical *Mediator Dei* of Pope Pius XII in 1947 both made strong statements emphasizing the importance of communicants receiving hosts consecrated at the same Mass. The Constitution on the Sacred Liturgy of Vatican II (#55) and the 1967 instruction *Eucharisticum mysterium* (#31) reiterate the point.

Sometimes at a dinner party, the food may run short; in such a case, the host or hostess may well rely on leftovers to supplement the meal. If the food runs short at the Eucharistic meal because of an unexpected number of participants, then a minister can go to the tabernacle for additional bread. And on some regular schedule it will be necessary to use the bread accumulated from previous Masses. In a large parish this might need to be done at one of the Masses each weekend, but it should not be done at every Mass. It would be good to choose a different Mass each weekend, so that the use of bread from the tabernacle does not seem routine to any assembly.

The common excuse for not following this principle is that it is too hard to determine how much bread is needed at each Mass, but many parishes, large and small, have learned to estimate rather closely. In most situations, the size of a given assembly will not vary widely from week to week. What is required is someone who is willing to make this concern a priority until experience provides an average number of communicants that can be normally expected at each Mass. Of course, if bread is used that can be broken into varied-sized pieces, then extra participants can be accommodated on the spot by breaking the bread a bit smaller than usual. If there is a quantity of bread in the tabernacle for the sick and for Communion services, recourse can always be made to that supply if the bread runs short.

Since we don't usually reserve the Blood of Christ, gauging the amount of wine needed requires the same kind of attention and experience. It is better to err on the side of excess rather than to have participants denied sharing in the cup. What is left can be consumed by the ministers of the cup at the end of Communion or after Mass.

The Logistics of Sharing Communion

After the singing of the Lamb of God and the dividing of the bread and wine, the presider is directed to place a small piece of the bread into the chalice. This ancient gesture was once a sign of the unity of the Church. In the early centuries, the ideal was one church in each city, with the liturgy led by the bishop. When growth of dioceses led to other churches throughout the countryside, the bishop would begin Mass earlier than his presbyters in other churches. A piece of the bread from the bishop's Mass was carried to each church in the diocese and placed in the chalice as a sign that all were worshiping together with the bishop. That symbolism is lost today, and the ritual is largely inconsequential. The prayer that accompanies the action is said "inaudibly," never out loud. So, too, the prayer for the presider's private preparation for Communion is to be said inaudibly.

The rubric says that the presider then holds up the host for all to see and speaks the invitation to Communion. Since we now share both bread and wine, it seems more appropriate to hold up both bread and cup as this invitation is issued, which is also proposed in the new Sacramentary. The text of the invitation can be adapted for feasts and seasons, though it should always end the same way so that the assembly knows when to respond. The new Sacramentary proposes three options for this invitation, and the *Sourcebook for Sundays and Seasons* (Chicago: Liturgy Training Publications) offers several examples of seasonal adaptation.

The actual logistics of sharing the bread and wine depend on the size of the assembly and the architecture of the building. A rule of thumb is that there should be two ministers of the cup for each minister of the bread so that all can receive both species without "traffic jams." Traditionally, a deacon serves the cup; beyond that custom, there should be no distinction between clergy and lay ministers or men and women. Both forms of the Eucharist are of equal importance; this might be more evident if the presider sometimes serves the cup and at other times distributes the bread.

The use of several ministers is intended to make the distribution of Communion more reverent and prayerful. Ministers of Communion should be taught to take their time and not rush the process. Each member of the assembly should experience this brief encounter with the minister as a significant moment. The minister should look each person in the eyes as the brief formula ("The Body of Christ" or "The Blood of Christ") is spoken. Some ministers have tried to emphasize the importance of the moment by saying "This is the Body of Christ" or "This is Jesus." The problem with such changes is that they distort the meaning of Communion. I believe that the official phrase ("The Body of Christ") is fortuitously ambiguous. Does it mean the bread is the Body of Christ? Does it mean the recipient is the Body of Christ? Does it mean the assembly is the Body of Christ? Does it mean that the recipient is called to accept the assembly that forms the Body of Christ? All of these questions can be answered in the affirmative, and ministers should not alter the formula in a way that restricts these multiple meanings.

Good pastoral practice includes periodic reminders to parishioners on the proper methods of receiving Communion. Many people still seem unsure how to hold their hands for Communion in the hand (one hand placed under the other), some snatch at the host, some who receive on the tongue barely open their mouths or extend their tongues, some do not respond with *Amen*, and some dip their own host in the cup, which is not approved (it is often unsanitary and sometimes messy). Gentle reminders on all these points now and then will contribute to a more reverent and dignified sharing in the Eucharistic meal.

After Eating and Drinking

After all have shared the Body and Blood of the Lord, the ministers should take their vessels to the credence table or perhaps into the sacristy. Any extra bread should be taken by one minister to the chapel of reservation. Extra wine can be consumed at the credence table or in the sacristy, or it may be covered and consumed after Mass. The vessels may be cleansed at the credence table, but that task might best be done after Mass. What should be avoided in any case is cleansing vessels at the altar during Mass. We would never think of doing dishes at the dinner table during a formal dinner party. Why would we clean the vessels on the banquet table during Mass?

During the Communion procession, the assembly should join together in song. This is often facilitated by choosing a song with a refrain for the assembly and verses sung by the choir or a cantor. The song chosen should fit the meaning of Communion, focusing on the unity of the Church in Christ, or it may be a seasonal hymn. Hymns written for adoration of the Eucharist at benediction are not appropriate. The Communion song is to accompany the action, not follow it.

After Communion, there should be a time for silent prayer by the whole assembly. Though the Sacramentary indicates that a song of praise might be sung by the assembly at this time, the importance of communal reflection after the Communion song suggests opting for silence regularly. Some people have resisted singing during Communion because they want silence for prayer after they receive the Body and Blood. While this may reflect an inadequate understanding of the meaning of Communion ("Jesus and me"), the desire for silence is a valid one. Providing a time for shared silence will allow all parishioners to enter more fully into the Communion procession and song without losing time for silent prayer and contemplation.

The Communion Rite then concludes with the Prayer after Communion, asking that our sharing in Communion might have an effect in our lives. This prayer should be proclaimed reverently, or it might even be sung as a fitting conclusion to this climactic part of the celebration.

Conclusion

The Communion Rite should be a moment of climax in the Eucharist. Taking care to celebrate this portion of the Mass well can enhance our experience of the Lord's presence and intensify our union with Christ and with one another, not only at Mass but also throughout the week ahead.

Questions for Reflection and Discussion

1. Does your community have the opportunity to commune under both species at all Masses? If not, why not? What steps need to be taken to reach that goal?

2. Do you see the contradiction when a parish refuses to offer both species while repeating Christ's words at the Last Supper to "take and drink"? Why do you think we are able to ignore the contradiction so easily?

3. Are the bread and wine used at Mass in your community the best that you can provide? Who decides what kind of bread and wine are used? Is it clear that this meal belongs to the whole community?

4. Does the presider share part of the same bread and drink of the same wine shared with the assembly? Can you think of any valid reason for a separate host or a separate cruet of wine just for the clergy?

5. Why do you think so many parishes continue to distribute hosts from the tabernacle, despite four centuries of papal teaching against this practice? What would be necessary to minimize the times it occurs in your parish?

6. Is the invitation to Communion adapted to fit the feast or season in your community? Who could prepare such texts for the presider?

7. Does the presider sometimes minister the cup to your assembly? Do you think this would be a good practice?

8. Is there need in your community to remind people of the proper procedures for receiving Communion? How could this be done periodically without seeming to chastise people?

9. When and where and by whom are the Communion vessels cleaned in your community? Is adequate care and reverence evident in the handling of the vessels before they are cleaned?

10. Is the Communion song sung during the Communion procession in your assembly? If not, why not? Is there adequate silence for reflection after all have received? How long do you think this silence should last?

CHAPTER 13

Go in Peace: The Concluding Rite

At the beginning of this book, we noted that the Mass, like any human celebration, includes four basic sections: a gathering of those who will celebrate together; communication between those assembled, taking a variety of forms; a shared ritual, commonly involving food and drink; and some kind of leave-taking or dismissal.

The two major sections of the Eucharist, of course, are the center two: the Liturgy of the Word and the Liturgy of the Eucharist. The Entrance and Concluding Rites are secondary and rather brief, but this does not mean that they are unimportant.

The Mass

In fact, the very term "Mass" is derived from the dismissal, which suggests that the early Church saw this moment of dispersing as quite important. It was not just a way to end the celebration, nor was it merely a way of saying farewell to those who had gathered, though both of those things were included.

The dismissal was seen as a true sending forth. Those who had gathered to celebrate the mystery of the Lord's dying and rising were sent out into the world to live that mystery all week. The Christians who gather for Eucharist are the same holy people to whom Christ entrusted the continuation of his mission. Having celebrated the wonderful works of God, especially those performed through Jesus Christ, each member of the Church is expected to do his or her part to carry on the mission of Christ, a mission of proclaiming God's word and of serving others in the name of Christ.

Our current Concluding Rite, though brief, is designed to make the same point. We are not just sent away; we are sent forth to mission. Each of the parts of the rite contributes a special nuance to our sending.

The *General Instruction* notes that, after the Communion Rite is concluded by the Prayer after Communion. "If there are any brief announcements, they may be made at this time" (#123). Then the presider says to the assembly, "The Lord be with you," and they answer "And also with you." The blessing of the assembly follows, and then the deacon or the presider speaks a formula of dismissal. The presider and deacon kiss the altar as a sign of reverence and leave in procession, accompanied by a final song, instrumental music, or silence.

The Announcements

Not so long ago, parish announcements were commonly made after the proclamation of the Gospel before the homily began. In our current rite, it is clear that the announcements are seen as part of the Concluding Rite. The reason for this is that the announcements are intended to point the assembly to the ways that the paschal mystery can be lived during the coming week. They inform the assembly of opportunities to live out the commitment that Eucharist implies, e.g., helping at the soup kitchen on Sunday evening, gathering for sung vespers on Wednesday, providing transportation for the youth group on Saturday, or visiting those hospitalized or confined by age or illness.

The *General Instruction* speaks of "brief announcements," reminding us that this is not intended to be a time to read the whole bulletin to the assembly nor to preach a second sermon. Most of the information that needs to be shared with the assembly should be communicated through the bulletin. Making too many announcements leads to diminished results: people stop reading the bulletin, assuming that everything important has already been announced, and people soon quit listening to the announcements themselves through sheer boredom.

A good rule of thumb is that announcements spoken at Mass should concern the whole assembly (or at least a significant portion) and should deal with information needed right after Mass or with something of special significance to call to everyone's attention. For example, announcing a bake sale by the youth group after Mass is appropriate, as is encouraging everyone to take advantage of an adult education series beginning that week.

On the other hand, it seems inappropriate to announce the time and place for the meetings of various committees or small groups. Such information should be in the bulletin or in notices sent to the few people involved. Of course, there are always exceptions to such a rule of thumb. If the secretary forgot to put an announcement in the bulletin, it may be necessary to announce it at Mass. But such occasions should remain the exception rather than the normal practice.

Those who compose the announcements to be read at Mass might try to write them in a way that makes clear their connection to the mission of the church and the Eucharist just celebrated. To say "All are invited to share the love of Christ we have experienced here by helping to serve dinner at the soup kitchen this Thursday at 6:00 p.m." is better than just announcing the time and place to show up. The more clearly these connections are made, the more the announcements will seem like an appropriate part of the Concluding Rite rather than an intrusion of parish business.

The announcement time also seems to be the best time for any non-homily talks promoting a special collection, giving the parish finance report, or explaining a new parish program or activity. This should not happen often, since the announcements normally should be brief, but a well-designed presentation can be seen as a way to invite the assembly to carry on the Church's work.

Communion to the Sick

Many parishes also use this time to formally send forth those who will carry Communion to the sick and homebound who were unable to join the assembly for worship that

Sunday. This also seems appropriate, for it is one way we extend the communion experienced in the Mass to our hurting or isolated members. This type of formal sending should be brief, but a short prayer over the ministers or a simple mandate (e.g., "We send you forth in the name of this community to share the body of Christ with our absent brothers/sisters and to remind them of our love and care") can be a very effective reminder of our bonds with our absent members.

The Eucharistic bread they take to the sick is best taken from what has been consecrated and shared with the assembly at that Mass, so that our absent brothers and sisters can share in the same meal we have just celebrated. The pyxes used for this ministry might be filled by the deacon or a distributor at the end of the communion procession and left on the altar until they are given to the ministers at the Concluding Rite.

The Lord Be With You

Though it is a common greeting and response and thus can become merely a routine exchange, we might see a special significance to the dialogue between the presider and the assembly just before the blessing. When the presider says, "The Lord be with you," and the assembly responds "And also with you," they are expressing a prayerful wish to each other that the presence of Christ might accompany each member of the assembly as they go forth.

By our sharing in the Body and Blood of Christ, we are reminded that we bear Christ in us wherever we go. Our communion in Christ strengthens us to be able to carry Christ with us throughout the week. This simple dialogue as part of the dismissal reminds us that we never walk alone and that our mission is to bring Christ to others.

The Blessing

The deacon, or the presider if no deacon is present, then invites the assembly to pray for God's blessing. The words of that invitation suggested in the Sacramentary pose a bit of a problem, however. They ask the assembly to bow their heads for the blessing. While this may speak a humble awareness of our need for God's help, it also means the assembly would never see the extended arms of the presider over them as the blessing is prayed. The Sacramentary notes that another form of invitation might be used, perhaps simply "Let us pray for God's blessing."

The Sacramentary offers twenty different examples of the threefold blessing (plus five more within the ritual Masses) along with twenty-six prayers over the people that serve a similar function. The proposed new Sacramentary contains forty-seven solemn blessings and twenty-eight prayers over the people. Planners and presiders should choose in advance the most appropriate of these options for the Sunday or feast being celebrated.

In addition to the options in the Sacramentary, additional blessing formulas may be found in the *Book of Blessings*. Some are appropriate to a particular feast or season, others might be appropriate when the parish focuses on certain ministries or individual needs in the community (e.g., for those who have just joined the parish or for new lectors), and still others are appropriate on most Sundays (see the additional threefold blessings included in Appendix II).

When a threefold blessing is used, the assembly is supposed to respond with an *Amen* to each of the sections. For this to work well, the presider must learn to pronounce the blessing in a way that indicates the end of each section, by slowing a bit and by the tone or cadence of the last few words. If the blessing is spoken well, the assembly will have no problem knowing when to respond.

The Dismissal

Because it is a direction given to the assembly, the formula of dismissal is properly spoken (or sung) by the deacon; if no deacon is present, the dismissal is pronounced by the presider. Three formulas are given in the Sacramentary, though it is common for the priest or deacon to adapt them somewhat. Taking a cue from the third sample ("Go in peace to love and serve the

Lord"), planners might compose a dismissal formula that is linked to the season or to the Liturgy of the Word for a given celebration. On Christmas, for example, the text might be "Go in peace to bring the light of Christ to all you meet." Or on the Feast of the Baptism of the Lord, "Go in peace as baptized members of Christ's body to make him present wherever you go." Or on any Easter Sunday, "Go in the new life Christ has given us and share the joy of resurrection with all you meet."

The people's response to the dismissal has led to much humor revolving around the reasons the assembly is thankful. "Thanks be to God" is not intended to be a statement of gratitude that the Mass is finally over! It can be seen as expressing gratitude for what God has done. This might focus on a variety of gifts. We are grateful for the salvation won for us through the death and resurrection of Christ that we have just celebrated. We are grateful for the word of God that has been spoken to us. We are grateful for the gift of Christ's Body and Blood in communion. We are grateful for the unity of the Body of Christ that is nourished in this meal. We are grateful for the opportunity to gather for worship and praise and mutual support. We are grateful for the mission that has been entrusted to us and that we are sent to carry out as the Mass comes to an end. It would not work to vary the assembly's response to make these multiple meanings obvious, but catechesis in the bulletin or in a homily might help people to embrace these final words with deeper sincerity.

The Closing Song

In this country, most parishes regularly end the celebration of the Eucharist with a closing song or hymn. It is interesting to note that this is not actually a part of the Mass in the Roman rite. This fact might remind us that there are various ways to conclude the Eucharist. The whole assembly might sing a hymn or the choir might offer a motet. The musicians might provide instrumental music to accompany the procession. On some occasions (maybe during Lent, for example) the final procession might take place in silence. Such variations might require instructing the assembly that they should stay in their places until the procession has left the worship space.

If a song or hymn is sung, it is proper to sing all the verses rather than to truncate it after a couple of verses. Hymns, like most musical compositions, are integral works of prayer and praise. They are not just background music to accompany the procession; they have value as prayer and praise in their own right. Planners should work with presiders to arrange for all the ministers to stay in place and sing with the assembly, only beginning the procession at a point that will match the end of the procession to the end of the hymn.

Liturgy and Life

The Concluding Rite consistently reminds us that the power of the liturgy is not meant to end at the church door. As the *General Instruction* puts it, the dismissal of the assembly "sends each member back to doing good works, while praising and blessing the Lord" (#57).

Those who gather to celebrate the paschal mystery are sent forth to live the dying and rising of Jesus. Those who share the Body and Blood of the Lord are sent to give their bodies and their lifeblood in the service of others, in imitation of their master. Those who hear the word of God together are sent forth to live that word all week. Those who have assembled as the Body of Christ disperse again to bring Christ to every part of their lives. Those who shared in the sacrificial meal are sent forth to offer their entire lives as a spiritual sacrifice in union with Christ.

There is no real separation between liturgy and the rest of our lives. We gather to celebrate together, bringing with us the cares and concerns of our lives, the joys and sorrows of the week past. We go forth after the celebration, renewed by the grace of God and the support of our brothers and sisters to carry the good news of Jesus Christ to the world. Like a heart pulling in depleted blood and pumping out life-giving oxygenated blood, the liturgy pulls us in and sends us back out revivified with the life-giving love of the Lord. Let us go in peace to love and serve the Lord! Thanks be to God!

Questions for Reflection and Discussion

1. Do you think most members of your assembly have a sense of being sent forth from Mass to carry on the mission of Christ? What would foster a heightened awareness of this sending?

2. When are announcements made in your community? Are they clearly part of the Concluding Rite? Do they help the assembly recognize the call to mission?

3. Who makes the announcements in your assembly? Are the announcements brief? Are they effective? If not, what can be done to improve their style and their delivery?

4. Who takes Communion to the sick of your community? Is this linked to the Sunday Mass? Are the ministers sent forth by the assembly? Do you think this is a good practice for your community?

5. Does your presider regularly use the variety of blessings available for the end of Mass? Who decides which blessing is most appropriate that day? Is it part of the planning process or is it just left up to the presider?

6. Is the dismissal formula often adapted to fit the feast or season? Does it function clearly to send the assembly forth to live the Gospel? Who might compose such formulas for your assembly?

7. What forms of catechesis would be most effective in helping the assembly to better appreciate their final "Thanks be to God"?

8. How often does your liturgy end with a congregational hymn? Do you sometimes end in silence, with a choir motet or with instrumental music? Would such variation be welcomed by your assembly? On what basis would you decide when to use each option?

9. If you sing a closing hymn, are all the verses sung? How can we help members of the assembly better appreciate singing as prayer?

10. What connections do you see between liturgical worship and the rest of your life? Does worship sustain your Christian living through the week? Do the events of the week shape your next experience of worship? How can we help the assembly to be more conscious of these connections?

CHAPTER 14

Was It Good for You?

Parish leaders who take seriously their responsibility for developing a healthy worship life for their community find that their efforts are not always appreciated or understood. It seems that everybody is a self-appointed expert these days. Every parishioner has his or her ideas of what worship should look like, sound like, and feel like. Their attitude often reflects what many people have been heard to say about art: "I may not know what is good, but I know what I like!"

Any parish seeking to improve its worship must be committed for the long haul. A solid tradition of good worship does not develop quickly, for by definition a tradition is something handed on over time. Worship patterns must be in place long enough for them to become truly the possession of the community of faith before we can really evaluate our efforts.

Good Worship

The first question, of course, is how to define "good worship." There may well be as many different definitions of that term in your parish as there are parishioners! The temptation is to evaluate our parish worship on the basis of how close it comes to our own mental image of what worship should be. If it has music that I like, then I judge it to be good musically. If the presider is someone I respect, then the presiding is done well. If I agree with everything in the homily, then the preaching is good.

One common manifestation of this tendency is the insistence by many today that Sunday worship should always make us feel better when we leave than we did when we arrived. A worship experience that leaves us disturbed or uneasy is condemned as being negative or unsatisfying. We want a joyful celebration that speaks only of God's loving care and makes us feel wonderful about ourselves.

Worship should, of course, regularly remind us of God's love, and there is joy in gathering with one another in the presence of God. But the presence of God also confronts us with the call to repent and reform our lives. There is more to the gospel and thus more to our worship than affirmation and good feelings. As one wit put it, the mission of the Church is to comfort the afflicted and afflict the comfortable! Good worship will do both, sometimes in the same celebration, sometimes in successive celebrations.

Archbishop Weakland's Criteria

If it is inadequate to evaluate worship on the basis of whether it makes us feel good, what criteria can we use to determine if we are moving in the right direction? In an address to the June assembly of the U.S. bishops in 1982, Archbishop Rembert G. Weakland of Milwaukee suggested four questions we might use to evaluate any experience of worship. I will paraphrase them here:

The *first* is whether the liturgy created in all the participants a sense of the mystery celebrated, a sense of God's saving love and presence among us. Were the people led to a realization that this was not an ordinary moment but one in which the saving action of God was present?

The *second* is whether the participants realized that they were part of a worshiping assembly, a people called together and bound together by God, not by merely human efforts.

The *third* is whether the participants had a sense of being part of a living tradition, linked to believers in past ages yet alive and life-giving today.

The *fourth* is whether the liturgy had some sense of the eschatological, that is, a hope not yet realized. Did the worship point us or draw us toward the future, toward the kingdom of God?

We might summarize these criteria as four senses: a sense of God's presence, a sense of being a community, a sense of tradition, and a sense of the future. Let's explore each of them just a bit further.

The sense of God's presence is what many people mean when they say we need more reverence in our worship. How we recognize God's presence and how we express reverence are further questions around this issue, but we certainly need an awareness of God's presence if our worship is to be more than entertainment or group therapy.

The sense of being a community also means a sense of common prayer and corporate worship. We still have a strong tendency to approach worship as an opportunity for my individual prayer to meet my personal needs. The renewal of the liturgy requires an awareness that the liturgy itself is Christ's act of worship which we are invited to share. We need to learn better how to submit ourselves to the dynamics of the liturgy, to insert ourselves into Christ's sacrificial worship, rather than to expect the worship to conform to our current needs or desires.

The sense of tradition also reminds us that the liturgy does not belong to us alone. It is a treasure we share with Christians of every age and Christians around the world today. While we rightly seek to link liturgy and our own lives and culture, we also need to be aware that we are part of something much larger than ourselves or our local community. We have inherited a great wealth of music, symbols, texts, and rituals. We must cherish the gift even as we modify it in our own time. Our tradition is dynamic, not static. It is a living tradition, so it constantly undergoes change and development. The challenge is to find the right balance between respect for what we have inherited and awareness of the constantly changing circumstances which the tradition must address.

The sense of the future also draws us beyond an entertainment model or a feel-good model of worship. The future to which we are called is God's future. The kingdom which Jesus proclaimed is already present in our midst, yet it has not come in its fullness. We are called to carry on the mission of Jesus, proclaiming the kingdom and working to shape our world according to the demands of the kingdom. There is an integral link between our worship and our mission, between liturgy and social justice, between our corporate prayer and the rest of our lives. Fr. Robert Hovda often said that liturgy was an exercise in "playing kingdom." For the brief time each week that we assemble for worship, we try to experience what life in the kingdom will be like when the kingdom has fully come. That weekly experience reminds us regularly of how God intends the world to be and gives us the strength to continue working through the week to transform the world according to God's will.

Evaluating the Effects of Worship

One of the common mistakes made in evaluating worship is focusing on a single worship experience. While that may be helpful at times to improve certain aspects of the worship, to expect one Mass or a single sacramental celebration to have dramatic results is unrealistic. Our worship is ritual behavior, and it is the pattern of worship over time that shapes us and transforms us. Liturgy planners and other parish leaders should look at the effect of the parish worship over a period of time in any attempts to evaluate parish liturgy.

We know the importance of pattern in other areas of our spiritual lives. We do not evaluate our private meditation on the basis of one meditation period. We know that it is the pattern and the long-term effects that matter. We do not expect one meeting with a spiritual director to transform our lives. We know that growth is slow and that the value of spiritual direction reveals itself over time.

So, too, with the celebration of the Eucharist. It is our participation over time in this central ritual act of the Christian community that will shape and transform us, if we allow it to do so. This is one reason the Church has always insisted that we gather to celebrate each week. It is not so much the single powerful experience as it is the repeated pattern of sacramental worship that has the power to transform us both individually and as a community. The Eucharist is sometimes called the repeatable sacrament of initiation. Through our repeated participation in the Eucharist, we are gradually drawn further and further into the mystery we celebrate, into the mystery of Christ's death and resurrection. One ultimate criterion for evaluating our worship is the extent to which it transforms the community into the image of Christ.

Evaluating the Parts

It is very important to keep the ultimate criteria in mind when decisions are made about changes in parish worship. The goal of worship is always twofold: the worship of God and the sanctification of God's people. If God is truly worshiped and the assembly is being transformed into the image of Christ, then parish liturgy is fulfilling its purpose. This does not mean that it cannot be improved, of course, but changes are only improvements if they contribute to that dual purpose.

In the practical realm, however, planners have to deal with less ultimate, more immediate goals. We can only move closer to the ultimate goal by improving the various components of worship. In this effort, the primary touchstone is composed of the basic documents spelling out the celebration of the Roman rite. These provide the norms against which we can measure our current practice. The following is a list of the major works that should be studied:

> *General Instruction of the Roman Missal*
> "Introduction" to the Lectionary
> *General Norms for the Liturgical Year and the Calendar*
> *Directory for Masses with Children*
> *Environment and Art in Catholic Worship*
> *Music in Catholic Worship*
> *Liturgical Music Today*
> *Fulfilled in Your Hearing*
> Introductions to each sacrament
> Introductions to the *Rite of Christian Initiation of Adults*

Circular Letter concerning the Preparation and Celebration of the Easter Feasts
"Introduction" to the *Book of Blessings*

(The first eight are included in *The Liturgy Documents: A Parish Resource,* 3rd ed., Chicago: Liturgy Training Publications, 1991.) A careful review of the guidelines and the vision contained in these documents will provide planners with a clear picture of the components of good worship. The book you are reading may be an alternate source of these insights, and the questions at the end of each chapter might guide a review of any community's worship pattern.

Planners should evaluate each section of the Mass to see what is solid in the community's current pattern and what could be improved. Because liturgy is ritual and ritual is patterned behavior, leaders who strive for good worship must develop goals and strategies for the long term.

Developing a Tradition of Worship

Every parish will undoubtedly find aspects of its current pattern of worship that need to be changed or improved. Such changes should be introduced gradually and with adequate explanation. Once the goals are established, parish leaders need to develop strategies that will lead step by step toward fulfillment of the goals.

Many Catholics have complained that changes seem to be introduced at the whim of the presider or planners, only to be changed again by their successors. Changes in the community's pattern of worship should never be determined by one person's taste or the whim of the moment. Changes should be organic developments that exhibit a certain consistency from one step to the next. This requires carefully developed strategies along with the patience to travel the journey of liturgical renewal one step at a time.

For example, if your community is currently not offering Communion under both species of bread and wine at all Masses, leaders should outline the steps needed to reach that goal. The first step would be to recruit and train new

Eucharistic ministers, so that you will have sufficient ministers to offer the cup without overscheduling the current ministers.

The second step would be to provide the assembly with a thorough catechesis about the reasons for the restoration of Communion under both species. This catechesis can be offered through a variety of media: adult education sessions, bulletin items, and homilies, especially if the readings of the Sunday lend themselves to such a focus. Of course, it is always permissible to preach on a part of the Mass itself: the *General Instruction of the Roman Missal* says the homily "should develop some point of the readings or of another text from the Ordinary or from the Proper of the Mass of the day" (#42). Such a homily should be given several times, because not all members of the assembly come to understand and accept such changes at the same time. It's a good idea to preach about the meaning of Communion in the Body and Blood of the Lord several times a year over several years.

The third step might be to offer Communion under both species at all Masses one weekend a month. This would allow the ministers time to test out procedures and movements to make sure that the Communion Rite will be prayerful. At the same time, it gives the assembly time to get used to the practice. Doing this much only requires a few new ministers, which will allow time for recruiting and training more. Offering the cup at all Masses on one weekend is better than offering it every week at only one Mass; otherwise, most of the parish will not become accustomed to the practice.

The fourth step might be to offer both species every other week at all the Masses. The fifth step, offering both species at all Sunday Masses, can then take place as soon as you have enough ministers trained. The final step would extend the use of the cup to all the parish Masses, weekdays as well as Sundays.

Conclusion

Evaluating parish worship patterns is essential to improving the quality of our worship. It is time we move beyond debates based on individual taste or nostalgic memories. Worship is the center of the life of the Church. It deserves our continual best efforts to celebrate as well as we can, for the glory of God and the sanctification of the people of God.

Questions for Reflection and Discussion

1. How would you define "good worship"?

2. Should worship always make us feel good? How prevalent is that expectation in your community?

3. How clear is the sense of mystery in your community's normal worship? How might it be made clearer?

4. Does your Sunday worship bind the assembly into closer unity? How is this manifested? Does the assembly have a sense of joining in a corporate act of worship?

5. Does your worship reflect a strong link with the long tradition of the Church? Is it clearly a living tradition?

6. How strong is the future orientation of your worship? Does it call the assembly toward the kingdom? Does it motivate members of the assembly to work to transform the world?

7. What long-term effects of worship on your community can you name? What effects would you hope to find in the years ahead?

8. How have changes in the worship pattern been introduced in your community? Do you think most members of the assembly understand the reasons for the changes we have experienced? Is remedial education needed about past changes? How would you introduce changes in the future?

9. What is the first issue you feel your community should address to improve your worship? What is the ultimate goal? What are the steps you might take to move toward the goal?

10. How can we ensure that changes in the Church's worship are based on solid liturgical principles and not on personal whim? How can we communicate that crucial difference to the assembly?

WORSHIPING WELL

Mick, Lawrence E.